MARRIED AND ALONE

The Way Back

MARRIED AND ALONE
The Way Back

Peter M. Rosenzweig, Ph.D.

 INSIGHT BOOKS

Plenum Press • New York and London

Library of Congress Cataloging-in-Publication Data

Rosenzweig, Peter M.
    Married and alone : the way back / Peter M. Rosenzweig.
        p.   cm.
    Includes bibliographical references and index.
    ISBN 0-306-44125-X
    1. Marriage. 2. Marital psychotherapy.   I. Title.
HQ734.R758   1992
    306.81--dc20   91-44333
                                                                        CIP

ISBN 0-306-44125-X

Insight Books is a division of Plenum Publishing Corporation
233 Spring Street, New York, N.Y. 10013

An Insight Book

Printed in the United States of America

To my Bobbie,
who has brought peace, friendship, and joy into my life.

With appreciation to our parents and teachers for their wisdom and guidance; to my sister, Sherry, for her support and encouragement; to Rivki, Josh, Rena, and Cheskie for their understanding in sharing me with this project; and to Barbara Segal Kohn and Heshey Fischler, whose technical help was exceeded only by their friendship. And to the brave people whose journeys toward intimacy I have been privileged to share.

And remember, we all stumble, every one of us.
That's why it's a comfort to go hand in hand.

—E. K. Brough

PREFACE

This book is for couples who value their marriage or hold out hope for what it could be. It is meant to inspire, encourage, and challenge you to examine what you feel about being part of a couple. It is written to provide company for those times when the path you are on feels unsure, crazy, or confusing.

Married and Alone: The Way Back is not meant as a substitute for professional help. Rather, it has been written to place contemporary challenges that present themselves to couples in a context of process. This book will help you evaluate the events and situations of your own relationship within a broader perspective. Perhaps it will offer some comfort and provide a chance for learning from the struggles of those who inspired it. It can serve as a touchstone as to whether the direction and style of your relationship is basically sound or in need of healing. Above all, this book is meant to be a supportive friend when you are not yet ready to talk.

It has been said that it is not so much the problems people have that give them trouble but the way they set about solving them. The chapters in this book present an array of struggles shared by couples in marital therapy. You will recognize some familiar problems and perhaps have your eyes opened to some unusual ones. More important, you will recognize the types of solutions that waste energy and life and, I hope, gain a sense of what approaches can be more productive.

In early chapters the values of personal wholeness and self-responsibility in marital relationships are explored. Some of the destructive influences of personal emotional "incompleteness" are traced. A view of how people can enhance themselves emotionally and bring a positive force into their marriage is offered.

The middle chapters identify both the feelings and needs that have central significance in a marriage. Syndromes such as the Competition Cycle, Shaming and Blaming, the Masking of Fear, and the Crisis of Trust are exposed as key hindrances to a couple's healthy development. Each is discussed with an eye toward discovering ways of healing.

The final chapters view marriage as a process. Topics such as in-laws, sex, children, and job pressures provide a background for the perspective that this process must be pursued rather than anticipated. Tools that can help you pursue the process are emphasized.

The book you are about to read presents three basic themes: enhancing personal wholeness, learning to blend differences, and viewing marriage as a process. All three can help to bring couples closer. In addition, clinical examples show how personal change can take place. These examples provide an inside view of the workings of marital therapy, offering couples alternatives to "lying in the bed they have made" and the all-too-simple message to "get along or get out."

CONTENTS

ix

Chapter 1

WHO ARE WE REALLY?
Finding Our Inner Voices

—I am black, but comely.

Song of Songs 1:5

This chapter introduces a fictitious couple in crisis. The partners are each undergoing their own problems, a circumstance that adds critical stress to the marriage. They know that they are in serious trouble, but they are confused about what it is that's causing them so much pain and unsure how to alleviate it. In this and the coming chapter we will trace how this husband and wife find their unsureness and confusion related to the difficulty that they, like many other couples, are having in hearing their "inner voices." The inner voice has much to say. It is neither mystical nor magical. Anyone can hear it, provided that one knows what to listen for. We will see how one's inner voice, if properly attended, offers clarity about one's pain and direction for its relief.

Rachel is a woman with an eye for beauty. She enjoys nature, loves to watch her children grow, and has a profound spiritual

gratitude to the Maker of all beauty. She has always loved life—
but lately has been feeling miserable. Her misery is related to a
distance that is growing between her and her inner voice. Dreams
of imparting to her family an enthusiastic sense of appreciation
for life now feel faded and remote. Caring for her husband, David,
and their four children has become an exhausting ordeal. For reasons she cannot explain, she is lethargic, depressed, and short-
tempered. While nevertheless continuing the car pools for the children, the night classes, and errand running, Rachel feels that her
zest is gone. What is especially confusing is that she is unable to
put her finger on exactly what is bothering her. She tries to keep
her unhappiness from her husband because she does not want to
burden him. Besides, her feelings seem to come and go. Because
she is a tenacious woman, Rachel does not give in easily to her
depressed state. Each day, she resolves to take a positive attitude
and to try to be happier. On some days her resolve seems to help,
but when the feelings of unhappiness return, they seem all the
more upsetting. Somehow, Rachel's old standbys of listening to
music, talking to friends, and shopping for a new outfit have all
fallen short. She feels perplexed about this growing sense of dissatisfaction and emptiness and is beginning to worry that her
crowded life is squeezing out the zest of her dreams.

David, too, has noticed his wife's emotional decline. He repeatedly asks what he can do to help. He remembers to bring her
flowers. More often than not, he offers helpful advice, which just
seems to make Rachel feel irritated. They seem to bicker more
frequently. There doesn't appear to be anything that David can
do. He, too, is becoming more short-tempered. Recently, after
another one of Rachel's sudden and unexplainable crying outbursts,
David went storming out of the house.

Rachel feels as if her life is unraveling and that she has only
herself to blame. "Maybe," she thinks, "this is all my fault. If only
I could feel content with all I have. Maybe I'm just ungrateful.
Perhaps, I should just try harder." Rachel's unhappiness illustrates
the effects of the "robot illusion" and the "emptiness syndrome,"
which will be explained in the paragraphs that follow.

COUPLES UNDER STRESS: A STUDY OF CONFLICTING RESPONSIBILITIES

Today many women have difficulties that are often the result of living in a state of conflicting and confusing roles and over-whelming responsibilities. Women worry about conflicting responsibilities and where to put their efforts. These conflicting responsibilities often seem to focus on the question, To whom am I most responsible? Husband, children, parents, home, job, and personal needs all clamor for a woman's attention. Many of my female patients struggle through difficult inner wars about how selfish or unselfish they can or should be. They struggle with themselves and often with their husbands about how accepting they should be of the expectation that they will put the needs of others before their own. If the wife wants or needs to devote more time away from traditional home and child-care roles, she then worries by whom and how the gap will be filled.

Often, in an attempt to fill this gap, women seem to forfeit their autonomy and individuality. They attempt to conform to the overwhelming array of external expectations in the hope that the pressure will stop and some measure of acceptance will be gained. In this way, a woman adopts everyone else's agenda—feverishly trying to be all things to her husband, children, boss, parents, in-laws, and self. Like a robot programmed to respond to the very next command, a woman rolls from one set of expectations to another. However, all of this robot-like activity—functioning as wife, mother, daughter, professional, and community-worker—is often both fatiguing and distracting. The woman is faced with setting priorities and keeping up her energy level. Our society possesses an enchantment with robots and seems, at times, to press women into becoming emotional automotons. Often the accumulation of diverse demands made on a woman results in an internal sense of distress, which can lead to "burnout." This burnout syndrome in a woman may take the form of an intense desire to escape, a weighted interest in fantasy, or a disenchantment with her husband coupled with a disturbing sense of emptiness. More important, this robot-like behavior distracts the woman from her internal process and sabotages her self-esteem.

LOSS OF THE INNER VOICE: THE SLIDE INTO COUPLE BURNOUT

One of the prices paid by women who are caught up in this robot syndrome is that they are distracted from listening to themselves. Rachel is unaware of her inner feelings and behaviors; nor, as we will see, is David in touch with his "inner voice." All of us have an inner voice that tells us what we genuinely feel and need, but listening to this inner voice requires careful attention. As psychologist James Bugental[1] has pointed out, it takes practice to hear our inner voice. In some ways the inner voice is like a muscle that must be exercised so that it stays strong. When women are constantly shifting from role to role or regularly challenged to refocus from being concerned for others to being more self-concerned, they can easily lose the serenity needed for listening in. Because they are often too busy and preoccupied to listen effectively, an estrangement from their more "true" selves results. They are so taxed by either conforming to expectations or opposing them that little energy is left to hear the nonreactive, "pure" self. Often, it is only in therapy that the tuning-in process can begin.

In addition, this robot-like reaction to roles and expectations creates another problem. When the roles performed and the expectations met do not feel genuine, they leave women like Rachel feeling a sense of emptiness. Some feel lost searching for a way through their maze of responsibilities, which may seem like a never-ending list of things to do. There is no place to stop and feel finished, much less accomplished or proud. "A woman's work is never done" may not be simply a trite phrase but a potential life sentence to an existence devoid of a sense of satisfaction. So, in addition to the exhaustion from attempting to fulfill all expectations, the robot syndrome also includes the painful symptom of personal emptiness.

Another factor that contributes to this feeling of emptiness is the loss of one's ideals. For example, a young woman may dream of devoting special time to each child every day. When she learns that it is impossible to have uninterrupted time for each child, let alone for her husband or herself, she may have feelings of incompleteness and inadequacy. When such valuable aspirations are lost in the busy flow of day-to-day reality, it is natural for a caring woman to feel a sense of loss or emptiness.

Additionally, whereas the robot illusion is caused by an inability to set limits, the emptiness syndrome is fostered by a lack of attention to oneself. When I ask my female patients how they care for themselves, what I generally hear, if such an activity even exists in their lives, is a description of self-indulgent behaviors that are heavily skewed toward maintaining physical appearance. The majority have no commitment to themselves or permission from their families for the kind of quiet time needed to reflect on what direction and behaviors will give more meaning to their lives.

Sometimes when women do take advantage of the opportunity to "listen in" to themselves but fail to hear a clear inner response, they feel guilty and without direction, leading to feelings of unworthiness and confusion. After all, how can anyone so busy with responsibilities still feel unsatisfied or incomplete? Confusion of this sort lends itself to dissatisfaction. Occasionally, women respond to the confusion by taking time out to gain a better perspective of themselves. Frequently, however, they simply resolve to "do better." This usually means an increased pace and yet more responsibilities. This version of "doing better" may fill time but not the internal needs that are echoed by the feeling of an ongoing void of increasing personal dissatisfaction.

BROKEN ILLUSIONS, PERSONAL EMPTINESS, AND WOULD-BE FIXERS

Confronted with the pressure of the robot illusion and the confusion of the emptiness syndrome, women tend to look to their husbands, mothers, and friends. Usually, it is their peers who can offer the greatest empathy, if not understanding. Mothers too often fail to appreciate the differences between themselves and their daughters, and many husbands tend to see themselves as "fixers" of problems rather than as companions. Being viewed as something that needs to be fixed can create more exasperation than relief for a woman. This is especially true for Rachel, whose cerebral husband overdoes the problem-solving aspect of his wife's distress. Husbands like David are unable to simply provide company for the emotionally strained wife whose needs include simple listening from others. Thus, the woman's emptiness and frustration are compounded by feelings of loneliness.

When I first met David, what I experienced was silence. In the beginning he was so frustrated that he could barely speak. Finally, he let it be known that despite his every effort, he felt he was a failure. His feelings of failing hinged primarily on his inability to keep his wife happy. David would feel less frustrated if he could simply dismiss Rachel as a "complainer," but her unhappiness and difficulties touch him deeply. David, accustomed to Rachel's joyful appreciation of life, feels himself to be an ugly spoiler. Moreover, he feels cheated: all his life he has taken great care to do his best, and now he feels tense, angry, and trapped in failure.

In addition to the anger, David is confused. His best has not been enough to make his marriage better. He is at a loss for what else to do. "I've tried everything," he said, "but things never get much better." Recently, pressures he has been feeling have developed into stomach problems. He cannot understand why he is not able to have a happier home life. Moreover, his recent arguments with Rachel and his attempts to help her out with her problems have resulted in even more frustration. "Why is this happening to me?" is David's most frequent lament. "I've gone to school, learned a profession, married a good woman, and tried to live an honest life. Where have I gone wrong?"

David now explains his early silence as an attempt to hide his feelings of shame. He is ashamed to admit how bad he feels, how sad his life has become, and how much he feels like a failure. Inwardly, he sees himself as a disappointment to his parents, to Rachel, and to himself. In David's own words, "How can I talk to you when I feel like I am standing here naked and exposed?" There seems to be no place for David to hide. His experience of personal ineptness haunts him like a dark shadow.

While David's priorities are particular to his lifestyle and reflect his individuality, he is essentially characteristic of many of the men whom I see in my practice. They tend to share a combination of personality characteristics and behaviors that hinders their ability to stay happily married. Chief among these features are hidden feelings of shame and hurt. These feelings are usually accompanied by behavioral patterns of false pride, sulking, withdrawal, and intimidation. What lies at the heart of David's problem is the fact that he is lacking awareness of these feelings and behaviors. Besides lacking awareness, he is also lacking the tools necessary to deal with what he is feeling. Finally, he is lacking the courage he needs to confront his struggle. Instead, he becomes increasingly mired in his growing frustration and unspoken shame and hurt.

UNACCEPTABLE LIMITS AND THE GENESIS OF SHAME

Once shame and hurt can be confronted openly, we often find these feelings seem to stem from extreme and damaging expectations. None of us lives in a vacuum devoid of expectations. We each have our own expectations to struggle with and additional demands placed upon us by others. Sometimes it seems to me that today's technological complexity alone burdens us all with an array of responsibilities that would send the most dazzling robot spinning in circles. Expectations may range from professional ones to communal, personal, practical, and religious ones: we must be successful, learned, pious but fun-loving, talented, concerned, thin, fit—and the list goes on.

Rabbi Joseph Soloveichik[2] once said, "By definition of the human condition, we are all in some way inadequate." One might add that experiencing inadequacy in any way is anathema to contemporary man; he seems unable to accept honest limits without shame. Moreover, asking others to acknowledge these limits is almost unthinkable.

How men typically deal with their experience of inadequacy lies at the center of their difficulty in marriage. Simply put, too many men don't know how to say "I wish I could be more, but this is all I am" or "I'd like to be more capable, but I did the best I could." As a result of this inability/unwillingness to accept limitation or failure, what wives hear instead is "Leave me alone" or "I won't be bothered" or "You have a lot of nerve to expect that after what I've been through today." What the wives see is angry withdrawal and brooding.

David's difficulty in taking responsibility for his impatience illustrates how ignoring limitations can result in feelings of inadequacy. As a child, David was seen as intellectually quick. He could look at pieces of a jigsaw puzzle and "just know" how they needed to fit together. Television had short-lived appeal because David could anticipate how the show would end. In math class David was the first to figure out the examples on the blackboard and would fidget until the next problem was presented.

As he grew older, David's quickness became a liability: the more he learned, the more impatient he became. While teachers marveled at his intuitive insight, they also complained of his short attention span. Friends would become uncomfortable conversing with David since he would impatiently finish their sentences for them.

Rachel initially found David to be incredibly perceptive; somehow, he seemed to know just what was on her mind. She was delighted to be so well understood and felt that she and David were "on the same wavelength." Over time, however, as Rachel's need to be listened to grew, she became increasingly irritated by David's impatience. His finishing her sentences made her feel dismissed or merely tolerated. If she tried to tell a story about her day, Rachel felt pressure from a look on David's face that always seemed to be saying "Get to the point already!"

David was not oblivious to the annoyance others showed toward him. Earlier in his life when peers would speak to him only occasionally or briefly, David simply figured that they didn't care much for him. Later, he assumed that others didn't care for his computer-like personality. However, when Rachel began to speak to him less frequently, David went into an angry shell, feeling unloved and personally unworthy.

Actually, David liked people and was interested in their stories. He was, however, largely unaware of his short attention span. The fact that he always played a mental game of quickly figuring out story endings or solutions had long gone unnoticed by him. In therapy David was given the opportunity to become aware of his short attention span and to take responsibility for how it was affecting others. He was able to stop trying to show others his understanding by figuring out their problems in record time and to begin learning to simply listen. Actually, David was shocked to learn that he could be valued for simply being a patient listener.

Many of the men I see share David's difficulty in realizing and accepting personal limitations, since few are able to take responsibility for their limitations without being crippled by anger or shame. The consequences of this avoidance are twofold. First, when a person is unable to acknowledge a limitation, the unreasonable expectations remain intact, often creating feelings of both guilt and shame. That is to say, experiencing oneself as not "measuring up" leads to feelings of personal unworthiness. Second, the manner typically adopted by men in response to feeling shame removes the possibility that their limitations can be effectively absorbed within the workings of the relationship. The personal tragedy of these men who live with a blurred sense of their realistic limits is compounded when the marriage generates further demands. Instead of one person living with internal dissatisfaction, there are now two. The couple has no easy way to openly confront the uneasiness created by the husband trying to be someone he is not. Often, the net result is a spiral of unhappiness, disappointment, and conflict. The husband is stuck with a mounting sense of personal shame, and his wife is faced with an increasingly withdrawn and sometimes openly belligerent man who is a disappointment to both himself and to her. Finally, the relationship is trapped in a pattern of unmet needs, hurt feelings, shame, and an avoidance that keeps resolution out of reach.

Couples who come to my office seeking marital therapy often-times are stuck in a downward spiral that is propelled by the merging of problems like those discussed so far. When the press of the robot illusion and the confusion of the emptiness syndrome of the woman are combined with her husband's unspoken shame and hurt, a pattern of mutual frustration and blaming sets in. Typically, the husband tries to "fix" his wife's schedule or priorities, a solution that further diminishes her self-esteem and competence. She feels misunderstood, still unsatisfied, and disappointed in her mate. Finally, the husband, unable to make it all better, tends to feel secretly ashamed. Behaviorally, he becomes either angrily disparaging or emotionally distant—or both. When a circumstantial problem the couple may be having creates its own pressure (e.g., financial management, behavioral problems in a child, or in-law friction), the couple may fall prey to blaming and bickering. They then suffer a decline in togetherness and trust. It is this spiral of difficulties that tends to push divorce to the levels it has reached today.

Chapter 2

HOW DID WE GET THIS WAY?

After years of working with families, I'm beginning to believe that there's no such thing as people—just fragments of families floating around.

—Carl Whitaker

After meeting Rachel and David, we are left to wonder how two bright, serious, and well-intentioned people came to be so unhappy. What are the factors that help to create the shame–anger male personality and the female robot–emptiness syndrome? How do these features give rise to the conflicts and the lost intimacy that make couples ready to divorce?

Part of the answer to these questions may be grasped by looking at marriage through a wider lens. Rachel and David's marriage is the union of two people. From another vantage point marriage is a meeting not only of different people but also of (1) different approaches to personal responsibility, (2) disparate methods of handling interpersonal conflict, and, finally, (3) contrasting emotional styles. This chapter will examine, then, how different styles, philosophies, and behaviors interact. Further, we will see how marriage becomes a kind of emotional crucible where these divergences are mixed and melted to support a whole new family system.

FAMILY STYLES AS MODELS OF RESPONSIBILITY

How people view personal responsibility is a key determinant of how happy they will be in their lives. We tend to learn models of responsibility from the families we grew up in and then carry these into our adult lives and into our relationships with others. One powerful way people learn about responsibility from their family is the way in which they leave the family. The family ethic about responsibility is often crystallized both in the terms of this separation and in the way families prepare young adults for it. Inherent in the message "You are now ready to leave home and be on your own" are values and teachings that define the transition from a dependent child to an autonomous, fully responsible adult.

Examining this transition and its relationship to personal responsibility styles, we discover that different family types teach different styles of responsibility. Helm Stierlin[3], a noted family therapist, points out that families have three basic ways of dealing with the children's leaving home to form relationships of their own. We will see how all three styles share a central and pivotal focus on the notion of "who is responsible to whom." The three family types are (1) the *expelling family,* (2) the *delegating family,* and (3) the *binding family,* and their responsibility styles are deflecting, suspecting, and inflicting, respectively. The expelling, delegating, and binding styles reveal the family's technique and needs. Deflecting, suspecting, or inflicting becomes the child's adaptive or learned response to living in that kind of climate of responsibility.

The Expelling Family

Life in the expelling family is like dealing with a bank that is about to bankrupt. Emotional and often material supplies are hard to come by, and the message to the members is "Get out as soon as you can." Frequently, children in such families are, in fact, sent away before they are ready to support themselves emotionally or financially. Often, they are expelled before they are prepared for marriage. Within these families, shaming, blaming, or intimidating may all be used to reach the goal of expelling unwanted or insupportable children.

The expelled children or young adults are likely to leave with the attitude that it's each man for himself. They are leery of forming close attachments and tend to wander not only geographically but in relationships and jobs. If they have been shamed into leaving, the message often perceived by them is "If you were really worthy, we would have kept you at home." Not surprisingly, expelled young adults have difficulty feeling self-worth and tend to derive esteem by being overachievers or restless daredevils. When they get married, they have trouble acknowledging guilt about almost anything. Their false pride and the accomplishments they sought to ward off criticism have much to do with this impression of infallibility. Their style of personal responsibility can be described as *deflecting*. That is, these individuals tend to deflect or put off the expectations of others. For them, responsibility is largely what they themselves determine it to be, and admitting fault on an emotional level is synonymous with being unworthy and once again being expelled. Distance, both physical and emotional, is likely to typify the expelled child's deflecting response to conflict at home.

The Delegating Family

While the expelling family seeks to push the child out regardless of direction, the delegating family has specific goals for its offspring. The young adult is offered a semblance of autonomy and appears to have been given responsibility. However, delegating families have conditions. Here, the message is "You are okay and you can lead your own life provided, of course, you dedicate your life to meeting our goals."

In delegating families the parents themselves usually have difficulty being responsible for the goals once set for them. As a result, the children inherit these partially completed, and usually unclear, goals. As the children attempt to achieve these goals, they often find that their efforts are either incomplete or insufficient. "Delegated" young adults are vulnerable to an ongoing sense that nothing they do is quite good enough: as one parental need or dream is met or realized by the "delegate," others appear in its place. Responsibility seems to never end, and the delegate is somehow always failing to "get it all done." If a delegating family's dream or goal is not reached, members harbor the belief that it is most certainly because someone was at fault; blaming behavior is especially common in these families.

Often the delegate gets married to either accomplish his or her final assigned goal or to escape the embarrassment of being a perpetual "not-good-enough" person. Delegates see responsibilities as a "crooked game" whose outcome is fixed. In their *suspecting* style, they tend to begrudgingly, fearfully, or cynically pursue their attempts to "finally get it right." Sometimes they reflexively adopt the goals of their spouse's family in the hope that these will be easier to reach. Identifying self-chosen responsibilities is difficult for these young adults. In fact, it may require a revolution in the way they see themselves. After all, it is not easy to shift from feeling like a slave who has failed to feeling like someone who is entitled to set his or her own goals. The delegate's sensitivity toward most any form of blame can make the give-and-take of marriage a difficult proposition.

The Binding Family

In contrast to both the expelling and delegating families, the binding family never wants to let go. "Bound" young adults grow up with the notion that whatever they do somehow controls the way the rest of the family feels. Acts of independence and sometimes even thoughts of independence are enough to provoke intense shaming. "Don't you see that what you are doing is killing us?" is a common phrase heard in the binding family.

When bound young adults enter into relationships, the rest of their family goes along, too—in body or spirit. The shame of leaving the somehow needy, helpless family behind is a constant burden to the bound person and to his or her spouse. For them, everything is a responsibility, except themselves. Martyrs for life, bound young adults tend to approach their lives without much zest. They regularly feel put upon, despite their tendency to be eager overachievers. Periodically, they may unceremoniously and without prior explanation dump or inflict unwanted responsibilities on their spouse. Usually silently resentful, they "press on," waiting for someone to rescue them. When they experience difficulty in their marriage, they hope that their spouse or someone else will solve the problem. Unhappily, the majority of Holocaust survivor families tend to fall into this category.

THE APPLE DOESN'T FALL FAR FROM THE TREE

David is a product of a delegating family. His parents, who lived through the Great Depression of the 1930s, had a terrible fear of being poor. As early as he can remember, David was conscious of his family's anxiety about money. That is not to say that money was a family obsession, but being poor was a family fear.

In order to allay this concern, David's father had a part-time job to supplement the income of his regular job. His mother was a full-time school cook. She clipped coupons late into the evening in an effort to save money. David mowed lawns in the summer and ran errands for neighbors to help out, but David's parents were not especially happy about his jobs. They had long made it clear that his "real job" was to study in earnest. His delegated task was to become a professional so that he would not have to worry about money and earning a living. In fact, David was often excused from family gatherings so that he could do his studying.

By the time David met Rachel, he was an accomplished professional. He had excelled in school, received his degree, and already spent several years in postgraduate study. True to his delegating background, David saw marriage as a mission. He carefully chose the tasks he could do best and proceeded to excel at them: he focused on finding the best job to support his family and meticulously performed his assigned household tasks.

However, David was not much of a team player. Used to responsibilities being delegated to him, David could take direction from his professors or Rachel but had trouble cooperating on a mutual project. As Rachel would say to her friends, "Just give David a specific job to do and he is wonderful, but ask him to help with the children on a rainy Sunday and you can forget it."

David's difficulty in working as a cooperative team member seemed strange to Rachel. She was from a binding family, where everyone did everything together. All her life Rachel had been taught that people must rely on each other. Since her mother had polio and was confined to a wheelchair, sisters and brothers alike would pitch in to help. No one seemed especially to mind helping out; it was simply an accepted fact that all hands were needed. Rachel, the oldest, would take pride in the fact that on Friday afternoon, before the Sabbath eve, the kitchen looked like a well-ordered factory, with each child preparing this or that.

When they first got married, Rachel figured that David's way of doing things on his own was due to being single and away from home for so long. As it became clear that he could deal with only one child at a time and became angry when asked to help make family decisions, Rachel's confusion turned to impatience. Later, as the family grew and as Rachel found that she needed David to be more of a helping hand and also a sounding board, her impatience turned into frustration and irritation.

David, for his part, could not understand Rachel's way of doing things from the start. "Why," he would ask, "must we discuss everything that must be done? Just do what needs to be done, as I do!" His analysis of Rachel's desire to share her thoughts was that she needed to become more fully independent and more emotionally mature. As the years passed by, the more Rachel seemed to ask for what David called her "conferences," the more impatient and reluctant he would feel.

From our outside perspective we can see how this meeting of family-learned responsibility styles created difficulties. But for David and Rachel it was a bewildering mess of frustrated expectations, and both felt stuck and shackled. Because David was chained by his "shame–anger" problem and Rachel was constrained by the robot illusion and emptiness syndrome, they were unable to resolve their difficulties. As David's anger increased, he was less cooperative, and Rachel's sadness, loneliness, and emptiness were overlooked in the fury of mounting activities.

Absorbing responsibility styles as diverse as deflecting and inflicting ones is only a portion of the mixing and melting that needs to take place in the crucible that is marriage. Couples also need to be able to adjust to different approaches to handling conflict. In the following paragraphs, special attention will be directed toward how couples approach and handle their conflicts. We will see how the tension created from the incompatibility of such approaches can oftentimes be as much as, if not more than, the tension in the substance of the conflict itself.

THE MYTH OF COMPLETED DEFICIENCIES: SPAWNING SHAMING, BLAMING, AND INTIMIDATING

There are myriad conflicts experienced by couples. One common conflict—caused by the myth of "completed deficiencies"— is especially noteworthy in that it typically evokes the conflict modes we will be addressing. This common myth, shared by many couples in troubled marriages, is that a half and a half equal a whole; that is, an incomplete area of development in one partner is somehow completed by the other partner. In fact, some partners are inclined to overemphasize that part of themselves of which they feel most confident, expecting, in return, that their spouse will complete their deficiencies. For example, a husband whose strength is his analytical problem-solving ability might expect that if he spends an evening planning out the family schedule for a week, his wife will overlook the fact that he was largely uncommunicative for the rest of the week. Or a wife may hope that her extroverted spouse's energy will overcome her difficulty in making conversation. Beliefs of this kind maintain a partner's weaknesses rather than challenge him or her to develop new and necessary skills.

This myth of "completed deficiencies" has powerful effects on a marriage. The noted family therapist Ivan Boszormenyi-Nagy[4] claims that people in families tend to keep a "mental ledger" of emotional credits and debits, using this ledger to keep track of efforts given and received. To some extent all of us take note of what we offer others and what it is that we receive. Often, when people have deficiencies, they expect completeness simply by giving more of what they do well. It is when this emotional ledger is poorly balanced that conflict surfaces (the tendency is to seek an equilibrium). Unfortunately, couples are prone to seek resolution of the conflict caused by belief in the myth of completed deficiencies by resorting to three especially destructive behaviors: shaming, blaming, and intimidating.

The following exchange is typical of the shaming, blaming, and intimidating that so seriously damaged Rachel and David's marriage. One thing that both Rachel and David have in common is their difficulty in setting limits on expectations. They each have trouble knowing the limits of what they can expect of themselves. This lack of self-knowledge is compounded when they try to address the other's expectations. This fight erupted on an evening when their needs collided. Rachel arrived home after squeezing a visit to a bedridden friend into her already-busy schedule; her visit lasted longer than she had planned. David, who had recently enrolled in evening classes to enhance his work skills, was returning from his first class tired, overwhelmed, and hungry. He entered the house and went straight to the kitchen:

David: Where's my dinner?

Rachel: It's still in the oven.

David: Why can't you have my dinner ready on time?

Rachel: It's not my fault; my visit at Sara's lasted longer than I expected.

David: (blaming) I have a headache; why couldn't you visit Sara another time?

Rachel: I already told you: she needed to talk.

David: So, I have to suffer with a headache all because Sara needs you?

Rachel: (blaming) Well, if you weren't so busy becoming the great professor, maybe you wouldn't have headaches!

David: (shaming) That's just like you. You can't keep your priorities straight, and I'm to blame. When are you ever going to get yourself together?

Rachel: You really are such a Mama's boy! Dinner is a few minutes late, and you are acting like a hungry animal. Don't you have any self-control?

David: (intimidating) This is the last time you are going to give me that Mama's boy business! If you so much as mention that again, you'll be sorry!

Rachel: (shaming and intimidating) Oh yeah? You certainly are a big shot! What are you going to do? Leave me? You can't even wait a few extra minutes for dinner, much less survive on your own. Besides, the day you decide to leave, you will come home only to find that I have left before you!

Shaming, blaming, and intimidating are forms of emotional blackmail. Their common goal is to force others to take on responsibility that often belongs to the person doing the blaming or intimidating.

PERSONAL RESPONSIBILITY: THE DOOR TO INTEGRITY

In contrast, healthy psychological development involves a sense of personal responsibility. Successful relationships thrive when partners view their happiness as being their own responsibility. When couples are unable to separate issues of responsibility, they raise children who do not know where others end and where they begin. Impossible expectations are followed by confusion, emptiness, anger, and shame. When the family's style of forcing its members to take on responsibility for each other entails shaming, blaming, or intimidating, the results are incomplete adults burdened by the shame–anger and robot–emptiness syndromes already noted. It is here that the ground is prepared for conflict between those who do not know when and how to set limits on expectations. This is not to say that those who take on responsibility for another—be it parent, sibling, or spouse—are endangering the relationship or themselves. Rather, it is the expectation that one must be the sole helper, that one is entirely obligated for another's basic emotional care, that contributes to the bitter harvest of the man's shame–anger syndrome and the woman's robot–emptiness syndrome.

Emotional style (i.e., how people take emotional care of themselves and others) is the last ingredient in the marriage crucible that we will discuss. Just as people have different styles in handling responsibility and conflict, so too do they have different styles in handling themselves emotionally; that is, they differ in how they deal with feelings and needs. Some people, like Rachel, keep their feelings and needs to themselves. They are not necessarily shy or introverted but tend to be private about their sensitivities. Others, like David, allow for a highly visible emotional profile. Still others can be open about some feelings or needs but not others. When one spouse's style of expressing feelings or needs is very different from the other's, there may be difficulty. Sometimes the shock that one's partner is either too loud or too soft-spoken overshadows what is said; the difference in style can often obscure the substance of what is said. It is almost as if one partner's emotional volume is either so low or so high that the other misses the message being broadcast. Feelings and needs are a person's emotional compass and sextant. When partners are not able to communicate their emotional "positions," they become like two lost ships in danger of collision.

As we can see, the ingredients in the marriage crucible are highly reactive. It is easy for responsibilities to become confused, conflicts to be mishandled, and messages about emotions to become garbled and lost. These factors contribute heavily to the strain on a marriage. Moreover, when a couple becomes frustrated and tense in trying to "mix and blend" their disparate emotional styles, it is all too easy for anger and despair to set in.

In order to work through differences and the inevitable frustrations, two elements are needed: one is patience accompanied by a belief that working things through is a worthy process; the second is a selection of tools and attitudes to resolve complex issues and to quiet the emotional turmoil that usually ensues. Our attention will now turn to some of the tools and attitudes that are necessary to keep the ship of marriage afloat and on its way.

Chapter 3

THE STRUGGLE: RESPONSIBILITY AND CONTROL

You can't have anything unless you let go of it.
　　　　　　　　　　　　　　　　—Sheldon Kopp

Responsibility can provide limits to the expectations that help produce shame by saying that only so much can be rightfully expected but no more. Responsibility can replace confusion with direction by delineating priorities and assigning them an order. Yet responsibility is a term whose potentially helpful meanings are often lost. What is the meaning of responsibility within marriage? If responsibility can alleviate much of the damage of shame and confusion, why is this power not put to better use?

THE HIDDEN HEALING POWERS OF PERSONAL RESPONSIBILITY

Sadly, when many of us think about responsibility, our associations are to tasks, jobs, and burdens that occupy our time. This perception of responsibility is a narrow one. A broader definition centers on the idea that we are created with a spiritual spark. Responsibility, in this context, is to activate that spark and to develop the unique qualities given to each of us. This concept is illustrated by the following story about the Hasidic Rebbe Reb Zusya of Hanipol, of blessed memory. It has always been a favorite of mine.

Throughout his life Reb Zusya, of blessed memory, had been eccentric. Despite the rabbi's apparent lack of Torah scholarship, his extraordinary character was held in great esteem by the founder of the Hasidic movement, Rebbe Israel Baal Shem Tov, of blessed memory. Numerous stories are told about people with special difficulties who were sent expressly to observe and meet Reb Zusya. When Reb Zusya neared the end of his life, the story goes, some of the younger Hasidim came to him and inquired, "Why are your teachings not more like those of Moses?" Reb Zusya is reported to have said,"When I get to the gates of heaven, they will not ask me why I wasn't more like Moses but, rather, why I was not more like Zusya!"

Each and every person may be seen as a combination of thoughts, attitudes, feelings, and behaviors blended together in a unique array. Fine tuning these characteristics to their greatest level of activity and harmony is both one's greatest challenge and one's greatest responsibility. We are accountable for how we struggle with this process. It is within the marital relationship that the task of developing our own uniqueness to the fullest reaches its greatest challenge. Two diamond-like souls are set against each other: their task is not to abrade but to polish each other toward a fuller realization of brilliance. They must blend their differing natures to a stable balance that can support and nourish a family.

PERSONAL RESPONSIBILITY WITHIN
THE CONTEXT OF MARRIAGE

Within the context of marriage *responsibility* has a particular meaning. Given our primary obligation to strive to realize the fullest development of our unique spark, a spouse's responsibility, then, is to help the other with that struggle. In order to do so, we must first have an awareness and appreciation of the special struggle undertaken by our spouse. Thus, marital responsibility means more than supporting the family financially or helping with the dishes, the bookkeeping, and the children. It means being aware of the emotional and spiritual struggles undertaken by our partner and providing encouragement. This is the essence of responsibility within the context of marriage, a concept that is both poorly understood and underused.

THE CENTRAL IMPORTANCE
OF FEELINGS AND NEEDS

At the center of the emotional struggle to develop our uniqueness to the fullest are personal needs and feelings. Needs and feelings are the warp and woof that comprise the fabric of human experience. To be responsible to ourselves and to our spouse, we must be aware of both feelings and needs. Our needs, both material and spiritual, give us direction. When we are hungry, we look for food. When we experience loneliness, we seek out company. When we find our needs and feelings difficult to manage, some turn to prayer. Many of us struggle regularly to define what we need. Often, getting our needs met by others is complicated by our not knowing clearly what we need. We may ask for love, understanding, or reassurance, but these responses are rarely given in exactly the way they are needed. Some people's needs are so basic that they can be met just by the mere knowledge that someone cares enough to respond. Other people's needs, however, are very complex and can be met only in very particular ways.

Having a responsible and clear sense of needs and feelings can resolve previously difficult conflicts. For example, one young man complained bitterly for weeks that his wife did not know the "meaning of love." Finally, he confided that what he needed was for his wife to be his ally against his brothers, whether his position in a particular situation was right or wrong. Irrespective of the "logic" of this need, it was clear that this kind of loyalty was just what the young man needed. In another situation a divorce was avoided when a middle-aged man finally understood that what his wife most needed from him was simply his willingness to sit by her when she cried. For her, this was a vital part of her grieving process for their lost child. Instead of becoming angry and impatient when his wife became emotionally overwhelmed, this man learned how to respond more specifically to her needs.

People rarely require their spouses to fight their battles for them or to resolve their struggles. Rather, what they need from their spouse is respect for their struggle and willingness to share that inner strife from which none of us is free. Some see the struggle with feelings and needs as a sign of immaturity or adolescence. Nothing could be further from the truth, for it is through the struggle with feelings, needs, and the decisions made on the basis of them that we refine our nature and build confidence. It is by feeling our feelings that we learn to trust ourselves and discover what it is that we have to offer to others. It is by dealing with the consequences of our decisions that we learn responsible and more realistic limits.

UNDERSTANDING EMOTIONAL NEEDS

There is another dimension of responsibility in marriage that deals with both needs and shame. When one partner expresses a need and the other either does not understand what is asked or no longer cares, there is a tendency to shame or blame the asker:

"Why are you such a complainer? Don't you know how to take care of yourself? Stop acting like such a baby!" The consequences of this kind of shaming behavior are twofold. First, the person being shamed closes up in the face of such attacks and learns that having needs makes one unworthy or not okay. Second, the need initially presented is left unmet, leaving a sense of frustration. Thus, shaming interferes with directing needs and blocks growth and maturity. How different this style of behavior is from the Hasidic attitude attributed to the Rebbe Marsham of Lubavitch, of blessed memory, who once compared people to many-faceted diamonds. His view was that one must learn to become a maven of the brilliance and luster of another's soul rather than an impulsive, disparaging critic.

To summarize this point, we can now see how losing the desire or support to struggle with our needs and feelings can cause shame and leave the marriage in a state of frozen frustration. Why, then, do some people approach the needs of others with disdain and shaming? One psychological theory points out that family members deal with each other's needs in a manner akin to the way commercial businesses operate, that is, by using a mental ledger to record debits and credits in order to keep a balance between emotional expenditures and receipts. According to this approach, family members, including the husband and wife, typically keep track of what emotional support they have provided others and to what extent their own needs have been met. When one feels that one is running in the red and that the exchange of emotional supplies is unbalanced, there is a tendency to utilize whatever pressure is necessary to even the score. This theory further suggests that people are rarely fully aware of this family process and that it occurs, crude as it may sound, virtually on a universal basis. Given this background, one can begin to understand how people, feeling that their own needs have not received sufficient attention, might utilize guilt or shame to bar their spouse from getting more of his or her needs met until the books are balanced.

There is a family pattern that serves to illustrate how complicated meeting emotional needs can become. Rachel, as we have mentioned, is a rather "other-directed" person; that is, her focus is usually on what others need or expect. Her "other directedness" or "external focus" can be traced to her early days in her grand-father's shop, when her main job was to be pleasant and keep the customers happy. One significant result of Rachel's external focus is that she knows little of her own needs. If we were to ask Rachel about her needs, she would most likely say that her biggest need is to have the energy to keep up with everyone else's needs and expectations of her. Lacking a clear "internal focus," or awareness of what makes *her* happy, leaves Rachel's feelings about herself dependent on her ability to continue to meet the needs of others.

Within Rachel's family this aspect of the robot syndrome has some complicated consequences. Although Rachel has trouble identifying and expressing her emotional needs, that does not mean that she does not want something in return for all her efforts. Thus, instead of asking David for specific responses to her emotional needs, such as finding "quiet time" to be with her, affirming her feelings, or simply listening attentively, Rachel's way of balancing the emotional ledger is to ask David to do things for her. Getting David to do chores has become a kind of substitute for asking him to respond to her emotional needs. It is Rachel's way of balancing the ledger or getting something in return.

This substitution of chores, of confusing material or physical needs with emotional needs, is not uncommon. (I suspect this thinking also underlies the peculiar habit that husbands have of buying gifts as a way of emotional appeasement.) In Rachel's life this substitution means that she, having given up on David's meeting her emotional needs, expects him to at least complete chores she asks him to do. More precisely, she feels strongly that David ought to anticipate chores and some of her physical needs without being asked. Moreover, asking her husband outright and directly to do things feels humiliating to Rachel. In fact, she said that asking David for help feels like "coerced caring." "If he cared, he would know I needed it done" is Rachel's way of putting it.

David is entirely frustrated by Rachel's attitude. He has always viewed chores as so many things that just needed doing. He was raised, if you recall, having everything clearly delegated to him, leaving little to the imagination. He cannot fathom the emotional intensity of Rachel's disappointment when he leaves some things undone. Further, he is bewildered by Rachel's hurt and fury when he fails to anticipate that some errand needs to be run or some task undertaken. Finally, David feels that Rachel is playing a game. Often when he tries to help, she refuses the help and insists on doing things herself. This reminds David of his father's "delegating" style: just when David thought that he had done what was asked, he found that it was not so. In response to Rachel's behavior David feels tricked, furious, powerless, and secretly ashamed.

This pattern of material and physical needs replacing unmet emotional needs serves to illustrate several points. First, it shows how issues of control and domination emerge when people become emotionally irresponsible. Because Rachel is unable to responsibly relate her emotional needs, she has fallen into a pattern of trying to control David's behavior at home. Similarly, because David is unable to express his powerlessness and shame in any verbal manner, he can only try to either give in to Rachel's controlling behavior and feel like a "wimp" or defy her and feel even more unworthy and ashamed. Second, we can see how lacking awareness of one's needs, not to mention the inability to meet them on one's own, impairs self-esteem. Actually, David is correct about one thing: Rachel will not allow him to help at times when she needs it most. Later, she revealed that receiving help makes her feel inadequate. She feels bad because she cannot meet everyone's expectations of her. In addition, she is also secretly disparaging of herself for not being able to meet her own needs. At those times when David offers assistance she feels as if her own inability to help herself makes her undeserving of his efforts. Accepting David's help also shakes Rachel's sense of being in control.

UNMET EMOTIONAL NEEDS AND "CONTROL GAMES"

What emerges from this discussion is the fact that when people are unsure about what they want and how to get a satisfying response, they resort to power games for control. Control is the opposite of responsibility. People seek control when they do not know how to struggle responsibly or when they get tired of doing so. Controlling also occurs when we are ineffective in negotiating with others to address those needs that we can't take care of independently.

Control is a tactic used when we no longer care to be responsible for ourselves. Its purpose is to force others, in any way necessary, to give us what we cannot otherwise get. In short, control is a strategy to pressure others into taking responsibility for us or for our needs.

The scenario that follows is especially common in marriages where a partner is unaccustomed to taking responsibility for his or her own self-care or needs. Typically, husbands or wives will literally wear themselves out in an attempt to anticipate and meet the needs of the other; then, emotionally, and sometimes physically, bankrupt, they develop the expectation that they, in turn, must be taken care of. Often, these martyr types know little of what they themselves actually need. They simply expect the other to make them feel good since they have done so much. Usually, when this does not happen, cries of "You don't appreciate me!" or "Look at all that I have done for you, and you won't even lift a finger for me!" or other such attacks are used to level blame in a wild attempt to somehow balance the books. Sadly, such people rarely get what they want, especially when they themselves can't identify what they need. Worse, the emotional storm that such control tactics create tends to obscure and cloud the basic needs that have gone unmet.

These kinds of blaming behaviors are based on the peculiar idea that responsibility implies punishment. People who are prone to blaming believe that if something goes wrong, someone must be hurt. Their logical response to this belief is "If someone is going to be hurt, better for it to be you than me." In other words, blamers take control by blaming others for fear that they themselves will be hurt if they don't strike first.

What is doubly damaging about blaming is that seeking a scapegoat does not solve the problem and togetherness is needlessly sacrificed. Blamers usually come from families where emotional outbursts greet any problem. Lacking the patience or skills to negotiate conflicts or resolve problems, these families use the simpler method of blaming someone. Children in such families quickly learn that it is useless to seek solutions because angry attacks usually drown out logic. The only way to survive in the face of failure or difficulty is to lay the blame on others before they lay it on you.

Besides the fact that blaming blocks the learning of necessary problem-solving skills, it also often cracks the bond between spouses. This happens when placing the blame for a problem becomes more important than the marriage. Marriage and other relationships are a process. Good marriages develop over time. They develop because the process of learning to live together is a basic responsibility that each partner undertakes. Blaming is a method of control that takes no interest in the process. No matter how much emotional distance results, blaming requires that someone must take the "rap." In this way, blaming ruins the morale of couples. Blaming makes the clear statement that the desire for togetherness is a surface commitment. As soon as real difficulty occurs in the marriage of one prone to blame, all that really matters is the need to avoid getting hurt or feeling like a failure.

Futile blaming in marriage can be illustrated by the following anecdote. A military platoon is sent on an important patrol mission. For this mission to succeed all members must return to base. However, when a member of the platoon makes a time-consuming mistake, the platoon leader decides to shoot the guilty soldier in the foot. After all, the logic goes, "Errors must be punished." The fact that all will be slowed down and the mission endangered is lost in the angry emotional need to punish someone. Couples who blame as a way to gain control inevitably shoot each other in the foot much of the time. They then wonder why the marriage is not smoothly reaching the goals they had in mind.

As introduced in Chapter 2, shaming, blaming, and intimidating are some of the most common methods of establishing a position of dominance or control. They seem to evoke feelings of guilt, unworthiness, indebtedness, or fear. Once the pattern of control is established, responsible struggle within oneself for personal fulfillment ceases and marital conflict and bickering take hold. The most devastating effect of this abdication of personal responsibility and shift toward control of one's partner is the obliteration of the positive attachment of love that was once there. The joy and excitement of seeing another person as he or she is, which is vital for feeling love, becomes lost in the desperation and determination that the other give what he or she is supposed to give. People who are caught up in the control syndrome have lost the freedom to relax and appreciate. Their only peace—and a temporary one at that—occurs when they have surely trapped their partner in such a way that their needs get met. It's hard to love someone you feel you must control, just as it's hard to love someone who you feel is controlling you.

This chapter has stressed the value of responsibility in clearing up the confused and damaging expectations that breed shame and in setting limits and delineating priorities and needs. In the next chapter, the reader will learn more about needs and feelings and ways to avoid becoming ensnared in the traps of power games and shame.

Chapter 4

TALKING AND NOT TALKING

Where can I find a man who has forgotten words, so that I can have a word with him?

— Chuang-tzu

Human beings are especially gifted with the ability to speak. Couples use talking or not talking as ways to let each other know how things are going. Speaking to one another, compared to giving nonverbal or physical cues, offers a more complete and informative message about what is going on. When a relationship is in trouble, the first step toward relief or resolution is talking. Talking, then, is the primary form of pursuing peace for most couples. Whereas touching, hugging, or making love may be more of a primary tool for some, even these important communicators will fail to deal successfully with emotional pain unless they are followed up with some kind of verbal exchange.

TO TALK OR NOT TO TALK?

Talking for couples having trouble is often difficult or impossible. For some, pride and a personal code of self-respect make talking about problems in a direct manner unacceptable. Commonly, these people experience the very presence of a conflict as a personal injury and might express this in words like "You should have known me better than that" or "You should have known that would make me upset." Others shy away from talking, fearing that it will create more problems: "Why talk? That will only make things worse." Still others remain silent out of a stubborn vengeance and a desire to get even. Finally, many times we don't talk to our partners because we don't know what to say.

Talking is, however, the first step. If you don't do it now, you will later. If you don't come out with what you have to say, your point will probably be made indirectly. Common indirect methods of communication are sarcastic gibes, broken promises, withholding affection, keeping physical distance, acts of inconsideration or noncooperation, drug abuse, extramarital affairs, and, sometimes, engaging a divorce lawyer. It is said that "nature abhors a vacuum"; when silence is used as a method of coping with conflict, the vacuum created is often filled with inaccurate projections and dangerous misunderstandings.

HOW TO SAY WHAT NEEDS SAYING

What is said need not be elegant or even necessarily exact. The idea is to say something about what is wrong and to invite your partner to add or comment. This mutual exchange is invaluable. It prevents issues that affect both of you from being ignored and submerged into quiet but destructive resentments. This airing out of a grievance and request for your partner's response is also the best way to prevent the indirect methods of dealing with problems just mentioned.

Statements like "If you loved me, you'd know what bothers me" are blackmail, copping out, or an indirect way of expressing anger or fear. "I have nothing to say" is a way of saying either "I don't want to have anything to do with you" or "I'm not ready to talk." Unfortunately, such statements provide inadequate information for the exchange to continue successfully. Their principal failure is that they do not clarify the source of the pain. They leave the spouse wondering whether the pain is the result of a specific hurt or the result of being overwhelmed and as yet unable to pinpoint what hurts. Those unwilling to talk or to explain why they won't talk are playing a game of emotional possum or of vengeance.

This chapter is written for those who want to talk but don't know what to say. (For those of you who think you might be stubborn, proud, or seeking vengeance, the next chapter, which focuses on feelings in more detail, might be more useful.) What we say when we talk to each other is popularly called communication. The word *communication* is perhaps one of the most used words of the last twenty years. It is also one of the least understood. Today we have communication satellites, communication media, and telephone communication systems, but there is still very little understanding of the concept in our private lives. In my practice I see couples wail at each other and talk about how they are not communicating. What are the problems involved in communication that make it so hard to achieve? Why is the feeling of being heard and understood so precious yet so difficult to achieve?

On the face of it, communication ought to be rather simple. We have two basic ways to communicate—verbally and nonverbally. However, there are times when one can engage in a verbal exchange and yet say "I don't think we have said anything to each other."

While some of you may be interested in reading about communicating and talking, others may be having a different reaction. Perhaps you share the sentiment of a patient who said simply, "Why talk? All we do when we talk is fight!" The plain truth is that many couples stop talking because their talks turn into ugly fights or pointless arguments.

BICKERING

I find it helpful to distinguish between several types of communication over conflictual issues as a way to separate useful talking from wasteful arguing. Communication over conflictual matters can involve (1) bickering, (2) avenging, (3) power struggling, or (4) issue confronting. The value in distinguishing between these kinds of communication is in recognizing how differently they are handled.

Let us turn first to bickering, which is perhaps the most common form of fighting between couples. Bickering is that type of fighting best described as "much ado about nothing." That is to say, when couples bicker, the conversation goes back and forth with no resolution. Although bickering is relatively harmless, it is annoying and usually saps couples of needed energy—actually, when couples bicker, they are often emotionally sapped before the bickering begins. Bickering, then, is a kind of nonfocused emoting. Two already emotionally and often physically tired people become irritated and deal with their fatigue by picking at each other. Bickering is a kind of emotional spillover of the response to assorted aggravations. However, since neither partner has the necessary energy to concentrate on what the issues are, the best thing to do when you find yourselves bickering is to stop and get some rest. Ongoing bickering will only lead to further irritation. Emotional energy and the goodwill necessary to identify and address real issues in a marriage are best not wasted on bickering.

Avenging is similar to bickering in that it too fails to address the real issue in need of resolution. When couples are engaged in avenging fights, they have long ago lost sight of meaningful differences and issues. Avenging is simply an attempt to "get even" and emotionally disable the other. Couples who become trapped in avenging fights would do better acknowledging that all they want is revenge, not resolution, and realizing that revenge has no victors, only alternating victims.

Power struggling is a kind of fighting that can be especially damaging because both partners are under the illusion that they are seeking resolution. Actually, when couples are engaged in a power struggle, what they are trying to settle is the issue of who is dominant. Each tries to force the other to be the one who must change. Like two mediocre heavyweight boxers, power strugglers push each other around ad nauseam. These people seem to feel that if they don't get their way or the "last word," they will never get any of what they want. While issues may be part of the power struggle, they are heavily overshadowed by the compulsion to win; in fact, when couples are stuck in power struggles, "winning" is all that matters. The belief that a reasonable or fair exchange can occur is absent. In marriages where power struggles predominate, trust gives way to a competition in which the winner takes all. The problem with power struggles is that they undermine any hope of restoring trust in a fair exchange. They foster a competitive climate that continually divides the relationship. Partners alternate between being winner and loser. Each lives with the strain of needing not to lose, neither feels valued beyond being a worthy opponent, and both partners continually lose opportunity after opportunity to care for the other.

MAKING THE TALKING WORTH YOUR TIME

In contrast to the kinds of communication over conflictual issues discussed so far is a fourth kind called issue confronting. What sets issue confronting apart is that it is the only kind of disagreement worth the energy. Confronting issues means that both partners know what they feel and what they want to change and are prepared to do business. While there may be expressions of disappointment, hurt, and anger, both partners are committed to finding out what the other wants to change. In these enlivened discussions it is not critical to find out who is right or who is wrong. Rather, there is the sense that what is troublesome will be aired and that both spouses will get some of what they need.

Disagreeing is an inevitable part of being in a relationship. Being patient and clear enough to disagree in an issue-confronting mode is not easy. Yet the more easily couples are able to distinguish bickering, avenging, and power struggling from issue confronting, the better able they are to conserve their emotional resources. The sooner they can spot bickering and take a rest, and the earlier they recognize avenging and power struggling and avoid the temptation to persist, the more likely that disagreeing and talking can be productive.

Productive communication is generally hampered by two other sources of interference: egocentrism and emotional illiteracy. Simply put, people having communication problems invariably either do not know how to see things from another perspective or have difficulty identifying or expressing their own feelings.

The Swiss psychologist Jean Piaget[5] spent hundreds of hours observing children at play. One of the observations he made about the games played by children under the age of eight is that they were invariably played without rules! In attempting to understand how these children could play games together without common rules, Piaget found that each child played by his or her own personal rules. This finding has always been instructive to me. Adults typically assume that they know what their peers are talking about despite the fact that we each have our own unique perspective. "You know" often seems to be a euphemism for "Who cares what I actually mean to say? I don't really care to be precise. Whatever you happen to understand is good enough."

Since it is my profession to try and understand other people, I am, at times, shocked and frustrated by how hard it is to even partially comprehend what life is like for another. Invariably, the culprit in my way is not just my difference from others but my egocentric notion that what life is like for them is what it is like for me.

EGOCENTRICITY: AN UNSEEN OBSTACLE TO UNDERSTANDING

For those who are skeptical about the power of egocentrism in communication, I offer some tests. One way to experience egocentrism is to relate a verbal message to someone and ask him or her to pass it to another, and so on down a line of five or six people. Watch for the egocentric distortions that occur. Invariably, the distortions are a product of the egocentric perceptions of the listener. If this sounds to you like I am saying that all people are self-centered, then you are understanding my point. This is not to say that all people selfishly or uncaringly distort what they hear; rather, my point is that, intellectually, we all operate out of our own personalized viewpoint.

Clearly, having our own perspective is not necessarily a liability. Yet when communicating with others, we find that for understanding to take place we often must make a deliberate effort to appreciate the words, tone, and importance of what we are being asked to hear. Merely listening to another requires only attention. To understand what we hear means we must actively concentrate.

There is an exercise I often use in group therapy that is particularly useful in facilitating communication. When two people are arguing or having a communication problem, they are typically asked to stop. Next, they are asked to limit their remarks to three or four sentences. After each communication segment, each person is asked to state what it is he or she heard the other say. This exercise regularly brings smirks to the faces of the group and bewilderment to the two participants. Usually, they will repeat the exchange several times with the same misunderstandings, and it is often only through the explanations of other group members that actual "hearing" is able to take place.

When you are having communication trouble with a partner, an appreciation of your egocentricity and your partner's can be useful. If you can remember that when you are not being understood by another or vice versa it is partially due to egocentrism. Hurt feelings can sometimes be sidestepped. There are times when we are not understood because it is particularly difficult for others to put themselves in our place. In fact, putting oneself in another's place is a logical impossibility. The best we can hope for is a kind of approximation of experiencing what it is like for another. Clearly though, removing the obstacle of egocentrism cannot be taken for granted—or even done without effort. Remembering the obstacle and the effort needed to move it out of the way may help us deal with misunderstandings with more respect and patience and less immediate frustration. I often think that if someone were to observe and listen to my conversations with clients in the office and the many questions I ask, they would assume that I must be a foreigner who is unfamiliar with the language. Yet it is the care taken to question, repeat, and restate what I hear that allows the difficult work of therapy to be done.

Affirming: A Way around Egocentricity

One of the practical lessons to be learned from the art of psychotherapy is the power of what I call "affirming." When a therapist restates in his or her own words what a client has said, the client tends to feel encouraged. Hearing our own thoughts, attitudes, or feelings coming from another, in the same way we meant them to be understood, gives us a sense of being valued or affirmed. Even when the other chooses to disagree with our perception, knowing that he or she took both the time and care to understand accurately may soften the discomfort of disagreement. So simply affirming what our partners have said by restating our understanding of it has a dual benefit: it can help overcome the natural state of egocentricity, and it gives our spouse or partner a sense of being valued.

COMMUNICATING FEELINGS

In order to further improve communications, or clear up misunderstandings, it is important to deal with feelings effectively. Feelings, especially intense ones, distort and color what is said. The same words spoken in the heat of an argument will sound entirely different when repeated after the argument has ended. Yet we all know that we have feelings and most people seem to know that their emotions matter, so why all the difficulty? I like to tell my clients that Sigmund Freud's contribution to psychiatry is the notion that people have an unconscious. I hope to be remembered for saying "People walk around unconscious most of the time!" What I am getting at is that awareness of one's feelings is a rare attribute. It is nonetheless a vital one for communicating successfully.

Without the ability to get a sense of your feelings across to someone else, only partial communication will take place. Probably the partial understanding that results will provide you with only a partial response to whatever you are asking. That is why expressing your feelings about the issue at hand is so vital to communication.

Oftentimes, I hear stories of personal horror or sorrow in my office. There are times when I will respond quite casually to these painful events. While some may see this as a nasty psychological game, my response often evokes a reaction of "You don't care about me and what I'm going through." "That's right," I'm prone to say. "As long as you are telling me about things that are difficult and painful in a way that sounds like someone reading the six o'clock news, I find it hard to respond differently." If you expect people to respond to you in a sensitive human fashion, consider whether you present yourself as a feeling person or as a cold robot.

HOW TO COMMUNICATE FEELINGS

Here are some guidelines for effective communication of feelings that may be useful. Clearly, before any meaningful or productive interaction can take place, you will need to have some idea as to what feeling you want your partner to understand. The feeling inventory sheets that follow can be useful to help put your feelings into words. Be as certain as you can that the feelings you have identified are your own and describe what it is like for you. Then, let your partner know that you want his or her attention and try to get your feelings across. Here are some ideas that may help you direct your communication successfully:

1. Don't attack your partner. He or she will only become defensive and will be too busy preparing a good defense to hear what you have to say.
2. Don't apologize. Apologetic people are rarely taken seriously.
3. Don't withdraw.
4. Talk to your partner but not about problems. Problems are abstract, and you want to deal with your feelings.
5. Look directly at your partner.
6. Begin as many sentences as you can in the first person: "I feel. . . ."
7. Keep your focus on your internal feelings and assume the responsibility for taking care of them in this exchange.
8. Focus on what inside of you is making communication difficult, that is, focus on your reactions, on the barriers you are putting up.
9. Avoid taking "inventory" of your partner or giving him or her a diagnosis; for example, "You can't understand because you're a cold fish."
10. Try to keep your feelings separate from ideas or opinions.
11. Stay aware of your feelings without confusing them with those of your partner.
12. Talk about what you are feeling now, even as you are talking and experiencing this exchange with your partner.
13. Limit what you say to the present or near present. Avoid long lists of complaints from the past.
14. Avoid nonspecific expressions like "most people," "the neighbors," "people in general," and "normal people."
15. Take a risk. You've come this far, so try to say what you want.
16. Finally, stick to three or fewer central feelings. Choose the ones that are most important, and put them into short sentences. The use of short and clear sentences about your feelings will make them easier to listen to.

Feelings are often difficult to identify even under the most relaxed circumstances. In times of stress and conflict they tend to blend into a nearly inexpressible lump in the throat. Here then is a list of the emotions I tend to hear most often in my work in psychotherapy. I hope it will serve as a cue to help diffuse the feelings that may become fused under the pressure of conflict.

FEELINGS INVENTORY OF COMMON EMOTIONS

Feelings	None	Some	Much	Feelings	None	Some	Much
Abandoned	___	___	___	Disappointed	___	___	___
Accepted	___	___	___	Disgusted	___	___	___
Afraid	___	___	___	Embarrassed	___	___	___
Amused	___	___	___	Empathy	___	___	___
Angry	___	___	___	Excited	___	___	___
Annoyed	___	___	___	Expectant	___	___	___
Anxious	___	___	___	Friendly	___	___	___
Apathetic	___	___	___	Frustrated	___	___	___
Apprehensive	___	___	___	Glad	___	___	___
Aroused	___	___	___	Guilty	___	___	___
Caring	___	___	___	Happy	___	___	___
Cautious	___	___	___	Hate	___	___	___
Close	___	___	___	Helpless	___	___	___
Competitive	___	___	___	Hopeful	___	___	___
Concerned	___	___	___	Hostile	___	___	___
Confident	___	___	___	Hurt	___	___	___
Contempt	___	___	___	Impotent	___	___	___
Content	___	___	___	Inadequate	___	___	___
Defensive	___	___	___	Indifferent	___	___	___
Dependent	___	___	___	Insulted	___	___	___
Despair	___	___	___	Irritated	___	___	___
Desperate	___	___	___	Isolated	___	___	___

Feelings	None	Some	Much	Feelings	None	Some	Much
Jealous	——	——	——	Resentful	——	——	——
Joyful	——	——	——	Responsible	——	——	——
Lonely	——	——	——	Sad	——	——	——
Lost	——	——	——	Scared	——	——	——
Love	——	——	——	Shame	——	——	——
Lovable	——	——	——	Shock	——	——	——
Loved	——	——	——	Skeptical	——	——	——
Mad	——	——	——	Smug	——	——	——
Mistrustful	——	——	——	Stubborn	——	——	——
Overwhelmed	——	——	——	Surprised	——	——	——
Panicky	——	——	——	Suspicious	——	——	——
Playful	——	——	——	Tense	——	——	——
Pleased	——	——	——	Trapped	——	——	——
Protective	——	——	——	Trusting	——	——	——
Proud	——	——	——	Vulnerable	——	——	——
Rebellious	——	——	——	Warm	——	——	——
Rejected	——	——	——	Worried	——	——	——
Relief	——	——	——				

Once you have said your piece, you need to do two last things. First, ask your partner to tell you what he or she heard you say. This has nothing to do with his or her reaction. Instead, it is a way for you to know that the information just sent was accurately received. After you are satisfied that you've been heard, ask for feedback. If you have said something coherent about your feelings, the chances are that your partner will be having some emotional reaction of his or her own in return. By asking for this feedback, you will both have a better sense of how you feel about each other.

A last aid in dealing with arguments and fights is a bit old-fashioned: say something positive. No matter how callous, cold, egotistical, or secure your partner may be, when a disagreement occurs his or her emotions are stirred up. At this time saying something positive really helps. Unless the goal of your fight is to get rid of your partner, saying something positive may help to limit the amount of distance created by the fight. A formula that seems particularly useful and effective is described by Irene Kassorla.[6] This communication, which I call the "sandwich," is a combination of three statements: the first and third of these statements are reassurances and the second is a criticism or a negative statement focused on the desired change. For example:

Positive: "I like talking to you and hearing your opinion; it's valuable to me."

Negative: "When you watch TV while I am talking to you, I feel uncared for and angry. I want that to stop."

Positive: "If you could stop the TV thing just when I'm talking, I'd feel a lot better and closer to you."

Or try the following version of the positive–negative–positive sandwich when dealing with an inconsiderate boss:

Positive: "Mr. B., I have been working for you for six years and I like my job."

Negative: "When you dock me for being late, I get resentful and feel like my six years of loyalty have little meaning."

Positive: "If you could curtail your practice of docking for lateness, I would feel better about the job and could look forward to coming to work."

When people are given a criticism in the context of a positive atmosphere, they are more likely to listen. Also, by using this approach you are reminding your partner of the value of your relationship and are encouraging him or her to help you to maintain its positive aspects.

It requires patience and an appreciation of the difficulty of overcoming egocentricity and emotional illiteracy to have true communication—a process that is much taken for granted. It is with this attitude that the aids that have been offered here can be

used most effectively. Remember, though, that the goal of communicating is not to avoid conflict; the idea is to have enough skill
to use conflict to better meet each other's needs. Conflicts offer
much to be learned. Couples who can learn what needs to be learned
in a conflict, without hurting each other too badly, have the opportunity to get closer and to maintain a comfortable intimacy all
their lives.

Chapter 5

WHAT DO WE DO WITH FEELINGS?

Man seeks to form a clear and simplified image of the universe, in harmony with his own nature, and to conquer the world of reality by replacing it to a certain extent by this image. This is what the painter does, the poet, the speculative philosopher and the research scientist, each in his own way. Into this picture he projects the center of gravity of his emotional life, in order to find there a peaceful sanctuary, free from the dissonances of turbulent personal experience.

—Albert Einstein

I have been emphasizing the idea that being able to express and master feelings is an essential skill for a successful marriage. Tension, anger, sadness, and guilt are some of the emotions that seem to give people the most difficulty. Let us now focus attention on each of these.

Of all the emotions that people experience, tension is probably the most common. Anxiety and tension both show themselves in a physical way and make us feel tight.

UNLOCKING TENSION

The stress that produces tension or anxiety may come from either unmet needs or unexpressed feelings. For example, when we need food or rest, our hunger or fatigue is often expressed in being tense or moody. Being in a state of high emotionality also produces stress and tension. Hans Selye,[7] famous for his work on stress, pointed out that tension may begin with emotions and culminate in physical changes. Thus, when we experience anger or fear, our bodies produce large amounts of adrenalin. This chemical's purpose is to get our bodies into a state of readiness to, in Selye's words, "fight or flee." Tension, then, if handled successfully, must be addressed on both emotional and physical levels. Within the context of marriage, tension relief requires that we deal with the duality of the emotions themselves and the physical "on edge" aspects of stress.

All too often, loud shouting, arguing, slamming doors, and even pushing or shoving become a couple's way of handling tension. This outburst of both emotional and physical energy does allow some of the tension to subside. The expense of such outbursts is, however, high: the issues that gave rise to the tension are seldom resolved; instead, a climate of barely controlled hostility is created. This entire mode of handling tension causes emotional, and sometimes physical, harm to the adults and inevitably builds fear for any children who may be present.

Moreover, a cycle of (1) unresolved issues, (2) resulting tension, (3) angry outbursts, (4) momentary relief, and (5) a reemergence of these unsettled issues is set into place. A couple caught in such a cycle seems to go from one emotional crisis to another. Being trapped in this cycle of unresolved conflict leads to a loss of intimacy. It may also result in hopelessness, an apathetic acceptance of an unfulfilling relationship ("This is the way my marriage is"), or the decision to divorce.

Reducing tension in a positive way means accepting tension for what it is, namely, a combination of physical tightness and an issue usually related to feelings or needs. This definition implies that tension can be diminished by exerting physical energy to drain off the adrenalin that has been produced. This can be done by exercising, doing some physically taxing work, or simply going for a long walk. Once the physical tension has subsided, focusing on the issues at hand merely requires some review of what has happened to cause friction. Often, a simple "processing" or talking things through is sufficient to close the entire tension episode.

ANGER: INTIMACY'S MOST DANGEROUS ENEMY

Anger is perhaps the emotion whose mismanagement contributes most directly to divorce. If couples were more skilled at handling their anger, the problems that bring about divorce would be more accessible to resolution. We can see this most clearly by noting that virtually all personal disagreements between people are easily subject to the emotion of anger. It follows that successful management of anger is a vital interpersonal skill. Anger can be mismanaged in an array of different styles. One common style of mismanagement is personified by the following example.

Michael the "submarine man" is an example of someone whose difficulty with anger became a personal liability. Michael was a rather taciturn, almost stoic, man with cold gray eyes. Internally, he was a tender mass of irritated sensibilities. Behaviorally, he seemed begrudgingly compliant to both his wife and boss: when faced with demands he did not like, he would offer a brief argument and then comply with an I-guess-it-just-has-to-be-your-way attitude. Secretly, Michael would plot and plan for those moments when he could "torpedo" the plans that had been forced upon him. He would patiently wait for a social setting where he could subtly embarrass his wife. In business he would await moments when his boss most needed his support and would instead offer criticism so astute that he could not be reprimanded. Much like the aftermath of a submarine shooting from underwater, only the havoc Michael created was visible.

No one could openly accuse Michael of being an angry person, yet both his wife and boss feared him. Each relationship suffered because of an uneasiness that could only be expressed in terms of Michael having "a lousy attitude." Behind the scenes Michael enjoyed leaving his mark on both these people. He openly complained that his boss failed to give him more responsibility and that his wife could be more loving. Only after some time in therapy was Michael able to realize his indirect manner of expressing anger. After learning to face his anger with others head on, Michael was able to gradually relieve their uneasiness with him. Dealing more openly and assertively with anger, he regained his boss's confidence and achieved a better relationship with his wife.

Of all the emotions that we will discuss, anger bears the greatest similarity to tension. Recall from the discussion of tension that both physical and chemical changes play major roles. These changes are especially pronounced when we feel fear or anger. Anger has at least four stages, the first of which is what I prefer to call rage, which is simply the first moments of anger, when we are so heavily "pumped up" by the adrenalin being produced that we are irrational and unapproachable. The common admonition not to try to speak with a person at the height of his or her anger is understandable; such a person is in the stage we call rage. It is not only useless to speak to someone at the point of rage but counterproductive as well. People need time to allow their body's functioning to return to normal; the adrenalin needs to be given time to subside. Once again, at this point any form of physical exertion is preferable to communicating. Sometimes, having a controlled, short-term temper tantrum is highly desirable. Pounding pillows or taking a brisk walk are clearly better than raging at one's spouse or children, which is, sadly, a common outlet.

Taming the Beast: Understanding the Stages of Anger

The goal of resolving angry feelings is not simply to redirect rage. However, if this vital stage of physical release is not taken seriously, further resolution is not possible. For example, in an especially emotional session, a woman confided to her husband of fifteen years that she becomes terrified when he is in a state of rage. When he then complained bitterly that she did not seem to care about his frustration, the wife replied that her noncaring attitude was purposeful. By this she meant that she was so frightened of his shouting that she simply learned to turn herself off. In short, the angrier he got, the more deaf she became.

Once the cycle of rage is broken by healthier ways of physical release, the next stages of anger can be addressed. One can usually tell that rage has successfully been diffused when feelings of hurt begin to surface. Hurt may first emerge as a feeling that one has not been treated fairly. "It's not fair" is often the first expression of hurt to be heard.

Actually, being hurt or treated unfairly is the cause for our anger. Anger is a way we can push away those who hurt us. Unfortunately, few of us have learned to say "I hurt"; instead, we get angry. But anger puts others off; it places them on the defensive. When people are busy defending themselves against another's anger, they are likely to be too busy avoiding being hurt themselves to notice the hurt feelings of anyone else.

In contrast to the wall that we put up with statements like "I'm angry with you," saying "I'm hurt" usually raises curiosity. "Why are you hurt?" or "What hurts?" are the most natural responses to hearing of another's pain. Rage closes off this openness. Reducing the rage allows us to once again come closer to the causes of the anger.

There is no anger without hurt. Learning to say "I'm hurt" without rage is an essential skill for marriage. How can anyone come close enough to help if you do not learn to say "I'm hurt?" Similarly, learning to ask "What hurts?" or "How have I hurt you?" are powerful ways to break up the wall of anger and return a relationship to a state of closeness.

The final stage of anger has to do with making a demand for change. Just as there is no anger without hurt, however hidden away it may be, so there is also no anger without need for change. This is true whether we are angry at each other or ourselves. People don't get angry unless there is something they want to be different. Any time I encountered angry patients, be they the most disturbed back-ward psychotics or the most sophisticated corporate executives, a demand for change was central to their anger. In order for the anger to be resolved, the needs reflected by the demand for change must be clarified.

The Vital Connection between Anger and Needs

Presenting needs enlivens a relationship. It moves the couple from the paralysis of fear or the repetitiveness of an anger cycle into the business of attempting to understand and meet each other's needs, an effort that helps couples to be at their best. Each partner's attempt to bargain, joke, or cajole for what he or she needs becomes a breath of fresh emotional air. Negotiating and a spirit of give-and-take teach the couple, again, the joy of contemplating how they can improve each other's life.

Sometimes, presenting needs and negotiating is not enough. There may be times when certain needs, no matter how legitimate they may be, cannot be met. We are all in some ways limited. Notwithstanding our love for each other, there may be things we simply are unable to do. What, then, is left to us when our needs are heard, understood, and respected but left unmet? One possibility is that the entire four stages of anger will be repeated. This is because one of the hardest levels for a human being to reach is one of acceptance. Simply accepting that, despite our feeling entitled and deserving of having our needs met, there are times when we must do without gratification is very difficult for most people.

The Struggle for Acceptance: A Clinical Example

Dealing with acceptance was a crucial aspect of the therapeutic work with Susan and Sam. At the age of fifty Susan had a stroke that initially left her paralyzed on one side of her body. The passage of time and gallant efforts by Susan, her husband, Sam, and her physical therapist helped Susan to regain much of the movement on her left side. Prayer and perseverance blended in Susan's life until she could finally walk again. However, she continued to have mild gait problems and much difficulty with her left hand.

Some months after the stroke Susan's doctors sent her home. They told her that she had recovered much of what she would regain. Whereas in the previous months Susan and Sam were an example of cooperation, teamwork, and mutual inspiration, they fell to bitter bickering and unhappiness. Sam, it seems, would simply not believe the doctor's assessment that Susan's hand would not improve. What's more, he was furious that Susan had stopped physical therapy for her hand. "Weren't the doctors pessimistic about your ever being able to walk?" asked Sam. "I never figured you to be a quitter."

Sam was a self-made man and the son of immigrants from Eastern Europe. His success was built on the credo that "one must never give up." When faced with anti-Semitism on New York's Lower East Side, Sam's stubborn refusal to yield kept him in business. Later, despite ridicule from his friends, Sam went back to school at the age of forty to finish his degree. Giving up was simply antithetical to Sam's entire existence. After months of struggling to revive Susan's deadened body, Sam was not about to give up now.

Mealtimes, in particular, became a time of horror for Susan because of Sam's insistence that she use her left hand. "Just try," Sam would plead. "Any improvement, any strengthening, will pave the way for future gains," he would argue. Susan, for her part, was overwhelmed: the months of rehabilitation had been difficult, and she was not used to other people fussing over her. Guilt about being so much trouble mingled with a longing for the ordeal to pass. Sam's pressing insistence no longer felt like support; instead, it made Susan tense. She became so tense at mealtime that she began having difficulty eating. Her tension level was so high that she felt as if she were going to choke on her food. Susan lost weight, her energy level dropped, and she lost some gains previously made with her walking. In short, Susan's entire recovery was being threatened by her tension.

In a new and more frustrating way this tension made Susan feel paralyzed. She wanted desperately to please Sam; disappointing him had always been something she avoided. Now she was worried about letting Sam down after he had "put up with so much." In addition, his impatience and anger were becoming more than she could bear. At the same time, Susan was frustrated with attempts to strengthen her hand, which, unlike her legs, seemed unresponsive to physical therapy. Moreover, hadn't the doctors told her that improvement was not realistic? Above all, Susan was emotionally "out of gas"; the ordeal of the stroke, being hospitalized, intensive physical therapy, and the energy needed to keep pace with Sam's expectations had left her drained.

Finally, Susan had to accept the fact that no effort she could make would improve her hand. She had reached the limits of her energy, and pressing ahead in accordance with Sam's wishes and her own dreams of a total recovery could mean she would lose what she had gained. It would mean more frustration with herself and with Sam, whom she loved more than she could bear. With the support of her doctors Susan drew the line between what she could hope to control and what was beyond her control. While this acceptance was without joy, it allowed her to more fully live the life she had. Sam finally was able to let go of his demand to have the recovery his way—but not until it was painfully clear to him that his refusal to accept Susan threatened to destroy them both.

Unsatisfied Needs and Emotional Maturity

We cannot always get what we need from ourselves or from others. The capacity to reach such an acceptance without blaming ourselves or others, and to do so without bitterness, is a hallmark of emotional maturity. This point is stressed in the following story.

One of Rabbi Moshe of Kobryn's Hasidim was very poor. He complained to the zaddik that his wretched circumstances were an obstacle to learning Torah and praying. "In this day and age," said Rabbi Moshe, "the greatest devotion, even greater than learning and praying, consists in accepting the world exactly as it happens to be."

THE DIFFERENCE BETWEEN SADNESS AND DEPRESSION

In contrast to the complex nature of anger, sadness is relatively simple. By sadness, we are referring to the natural sense of pain that we experience in the face of loss. It is important to note that such a feeling of sadness is different from depression, which is built up over time. A sad person may become depressed when the loss that preceded the sadness is not properly mourned. Prolonged states of sadness and longstanding unresolved anger are two primary psychological causes of depression.

Sadness tends to pass when people are permitted the time and autonomy to mourn their losses in their own personal way. Allowing others to go through their sadness at a pace comfortable for them is often the most loving response you can give. It is when others interfere with natural mourning that sadness becomes a problem for couples. I have seen relationships destroyed by one partner being unable to tolerate the other's sadness and to share in it.

An example of relationships destroyed by an inability to tolerate mourning involves Marty and his family. Marty was an only child. His parents were survivors of the Holocaust. These factors made Marty's struggle with mourning especially difficult. From his youth he had known that his parents were the only ones of their family to come out of Europe alive. Marty had a strong sense of history and deep feelings about his parents' survival. While schoolmates dreamed of money and professional accomplishment, Marty dreamed about having a large family.

I met Marty after his son Adam died. Although he and his wife, Rose, were both young enough to have more children, Marty was psychologically devastated. Adam had had a lengthy illness, and Marty felt that he had failed to cure his son. In many ways Marty's perception of Adam's death had more to do with a fantasy of failing to save him from phantom Nazi soldiers than failing to stop the progress of an incurable leukemia.

Failure and defeat were Marty's gut reactions to Adam's death. Both these feelings left Marty with a wall of anger that blocked the path to mourning and acceptance. He was furious at his own helplessness and enraged that neither the doctors nor God would save Adam. Fury gave way to desperation and mistrust. For months Marty's depression grew. His performance at work declined, and the closeness between Marty and Rose deteriorated. Marty could not articulate his private war to Rose. When Rose would plead that they go on with their lives, Marty felt she was being disloyal. Sometimes days at a time would go by without Marty saying a word to his wife. Nothing he did say seemed to open the door to allow others to see or take in his personal purgatory. He felt furious at what he saw as Rose's betrayal of him; he felt alone in his mourning. His sense of humor seemed to disappear, and friends began teasing him about being a hermit. He retaliated by refusing to receive their visits or phone calls. Spiritually, Marty had become a stone. He admitted that he wanted none of God's help for himself and that bitterness about Adam had poisoned his faith. Marty had allowed death to nearly destroy his marriage, friendships, and career. When he finally entered therapy, he was emotionally, spiritually, and physically beaten.

Sharing Sadness

The inability to empathize with the sadness of a spouse can destroy the relationship. One couple I encountered had experienced a miscarriage, another a stillborn child. In both cases the lack of support and refusal to allow feelings of sadness resulted in divorce. In one case the wife was never able to forgive her husband for minimizing her pain; in the other the husband was not able to overcome the distance he experienced when his wife became angry with his "incessant" crying for his unborn daughter.

At the heart of coping with sadness is understanding the difference between loss and self-pity, or defeat. A Hasidic story illustrates this well: Two people lost their homes to fire. Upon returning to the ashes, both wept. One wept, cried out, and wept some more. The other wept too, but with tears still streaming down his face he replaced one brick. Then he cried some more and replaced another.

As partners and witnesses to the inevitable losses our spouses will experience, we are charged with the responsibility to allow for sadness and periods of feeling loss. However, life challenges one to smile through tears. We need to be able to carry on in a spirit of hope and acceptance. Usually, this does not occur until the mourning cycle has been completed. Denial of all feelings, isolation, trying to bargain away the loss, depression, and acceptance are all normal parts of the mourning cycle. It is only when mourning evolves into an attitude of defeat that we need to become concerned about how our spouse is adjusting. This occurs when the process of mourning remains incomplete and mourning becomes a permanent unhappy lifestyle.

UNRAVELING THE GUILT CYCLE

Guilt is a feeling whose complexity and destructive potential make it more similar to anger than to sadness. In addition, guilt, like anger, can paralyze a relationship and freeze the vital exchange of feelings and needs. This is because the partners become polarized in the roles of tyrant and victim, just as they do with anger. In dealing with guilt, one partner becomes the "righteous one" while the other is stuck being the guilty or "bad one."

Eli and Linda were caught up in the "always good/always bad" cycle we are considering. Eli was someone who had returned to his Jewish faith (a *baal teshuvah*). He had grown up in a secular household where religion was viewed as a combination of misinformation and superstition. During his college years Eli took some philosophy classes and became interested in religion. Ultimately, he took on a traditional Jewish lifestyle.

Linda, in contrast, had grown up in a devout family. Not only were her parents steeped in the observance of tradition but several of her uncles were well-known teachers and Jewish scholars. Linda had a broad and deep understanding of Jewish law and observance. She had been a conscientious student, enhancing her family background by scholarship of her own.

When Eli and Linda met, they shared a deep intellectual attraction. Eli was in awe of Linda's apparent command of anything Jewish. In his eyes she was an encyclopedia of knowledge and a "walking–talking" piece of Jewish culture. She spoke both Hebrew and Yiddish, could cook Jewish foods, and knew many prayers and a seemingly endless number of Jewish songs by heart. Eli, on the other hand, had just begun to recognize Hebrew letters, knew nothing but some slang in Yiddish, and was just beginning to learn about Jewish law and custom. By his own description Eli had been raised a "gastronomic Jew": his greatest familiarity with Judaism was through the food he had eaten at home and at the neighborhood deli.

Linda was taken by Eli's passion for Jewish identity. His energy and perseverance at learning his lost tradition had earned Eli something of a reputation at school. In order to broaden his understanding of Judaism he would cast pride and comfort aside and ask questions until he felt he understood, ignoring both his professor's impatience and the questioning glances of his fellow students. At times he would turn night into day, furiously reviewing and researching what he had learned. To Linda, Eli was like a modern-day Rabbi Akiva, a giant among Jewish scholars who began to study Torah at the age of forty.

When Eli and Linda married, there were those who saw them as a romance come true. In fact, there was much joy and a happy sense of belonging together that filled this relationship. Much of the time Linda and Eli were able to enjoy their mutual appreciation of each other. It was, however, at times of conflict that Linda and Eli got caught in a destructive pattern in which Linda was somehow always in the right while Eli was somehow always in the wrong. While some of this pattern was attributable to the fact that Linda knew more about how to run an observant Jewish home than did

Eli, it was also true that Linda had a hard time being wrong about anything.

In Linda's own family, having the right information was a high priority; having the right answer was a prerequisite for respect. Early on, Linda saw that to earn the attention of the men in her family, it was important to be right; unfortunately, in her own mind, being wrong was reason for feeling shame. Linda, for instance, would squirm in sympathy when her dad would quiz her brothers and chide them if their answers were incorrect.

Linda's compulsion to be right was to have a severe impact on her husband. In the early stages of the marriage Eli was pleased when Linda would correct errors made due to his inexperience or ignorance. However, as his own fund of knowledge increased and he argued with Linda, he found that she rarely conceded a point. Eli found this annoying. Later, he would become openly angry, only to have Linda berate him for having a nasty temper. Eli started to feel defeated, beaten down, and not good enough for Linda. The more Linda was right, the less Eli thought of himself. He felt increasingly guilty about making Linda so unhappy. He questioned the progress of his Jewish studies and secretly thought that Linda would have been happier with someone on her own level. His self-esteem suffered because he felt that he would never emerge as the leader of his own family. In the end, Eli gave up his pursuit of Jewish studies and divorced Linda.

Linda worried about the unresolved arguments and the conflict that marked the last months of marriage and about Eli's open resentment. She hoped that he would see the wisdom in her points of view and stop the bickering. Because she was so consumed by the need to be right, Linda was unaware of the toll this was taking on Eli's self-esteem. When Eli told her he wanted a divorce, Linda was shocked. She was sure Eli was wrong about the divorce and his reasons for it. The inability to move from polarized positions, where Linda was "good" and "right" and Eli was "bad" and "wrong," ultimately was the undoing of this relationship.

While some marriages maintain this pattern of a righteous spouse and an evil one for years, the price to be paid is a breakdown in the exchange of feelings and needs. Each partner is, in effect, stuck: one is always beyond reproach and improvement while the other can never really do anything right. The result of such a pattern is a cessation of the meaningful exchange of feelings and needs, a growing resentment, and the creation of an atmosphere colored by extremes. That is, the family ethic becomes one of good and bad or black and white. When guilt patterns are operative, people are never seen in their complexity: there are no in-betweens, only the extremes of good and bad. Ultimately, after the inevitable resentment and dissatisfaction that such thinking perpetuates, hopelessness sets in. These factors, when combined, produce a climate for divorce. In these cases, divorce is merely the formal end to a relationship whose life's breath was long ago sucked out by the guilt process.

An illustration of how guilt almost destroyed a relationship can be seen in the case of Frank and Debbie. Both had been married before: Frank's wife had died suddenly of a heart attack, and Debbie and her husband were divorced after some twenty years of unhappiness. What especially attracted Debbie to Frank was her perception of him as mature, bright, and a "take charge" sort of a person, qualities very much the opposite of her ex-husband's. Frank, for his part, was pleased to have a companion, especially one who was as appreciative of his efforts as Debbie was.

After they had been married for about three years, Frank experienced his first serious business failure. With that failure he sank into a depression, not unlike the one he suffered after his wife's death. What complicated his response was the fact that Frank was also immobilized by guilt: he felt that he had let Debbie down. In fact, Frank became obsessed with the feeling that he was an absolute failure. Debbie, for her part, was shaken by both the economic losses and Frank's depression. Her love and trust in him had been largely based on his being the only reliable and strong man she had ever known. She couldn't understand how such drastic changes had happened. In addition, she was angry at Frank for letting her down and upset with herself for trusting another man.

Frank's way of reacting to Debbie's anger and disappointment was to accept the expectation that he be able to recover immediately and completely, both financially and emotionally. He would launch into harangues of self-contempt for letting Debbie down and insist that he should be able to do better more quickly. The more insistent Frank became that he meet these self-imposed expectations, the more he fed the guilt cycle. What's more, the more Debbie showed anger and disappointment, the greater was Frank's impatience with himself and guilt. Not surprisingly, he also sank deeper into depression. In addition, Frank was becoming so verbally self-abusive that he was unpleasant to be around and nasty to anyone who tried to help.

Actually, it was Debbie who finally helped Frank out of the guilt cycle. After taking a hard look at the real differences between Frank and her ineffectual ex-husband, she became sure that Frank would somehow pull through. Her initial panic now gone, Debbie chided Frank about his unrealistic expectations and admitted that she had found her own to be similarly unrealistic. "Frank," she said, "it's nonsense to expect to put this all together so quickly. Besides, if you insist on doing this all at such an intense pace, all you are going to do is drive us both crazy. Listen to me," she said, "I know that you will get back on your feet. You have been a successful businessman for twenty years. I'm sure you will manage to provide for me. Stop concentrating so much on the failure and try to treat yourself and me more pleasantly. For right now that is all I want."

With Debbie's reassurance, Frank was able to begin unhooking himself from the goal of turning disaster into instant success. He stopped his furious writing of new sales campaigns and began to focus on what he could do to meet Debbie's newly stated need. Once out of the tunnel walled in by guilt and depression from which he believed an instant financial windfall was his only escape, Frank began to look for ways he could be more pleasant to Debbie and less tense when they were together. He worked at the relaxation exercises he had previously disdained as nonsense. Reading books, listening to music, and taking walks gradually replaced sitting and brooding. In short, as Frank moved away from his own and from Debbie's initial and unreasonable expectation, he was free to respond to her and their situation in a more positive and productive way.

The reader will recall our earlier discussion in which an accounting system of relationships was described. Briefly, it was mentioned how we all keep an internal, often unconscious, account of emotional energies spent and of those received in return. It is perhaps against this background of emotional debits and credits that guilt may best be examined. Simply, guilt is the experience of feeling that we owe someone something.

Demands and Guilt: Having One without the Other

Guilt begins with the presentation of a demand that we perceive as being either unrealistic or unacceptable. Owing someone, in itself, does not produce guilt. On the contrary, there are personal and relationship benefits that are the result of being able to repay an emotional debt: we feel good about ourselves and others when we can repay a kindness or return a favor. It is when the exchange feels unrealistic or unacceptable that guilt emerges. Whether the demand is made by others or we make it of ourselves, an unreasonable demand is necessary for the guilt process to begin. Unrealistic expectations create a gap between what we genuinely have to offer and what is expected. The presence of such gaps threatens self-esteem. The gaping distance between what others think we ought to be offering them and what we are prepared to give creates tension. There is a natural tendency to fill the gap, complete the gestalt, and relieve this tension that I call "guilt." In the face of an unacceptable or unrealistic demand, people slide into a series of reactions that I call the "guilt cycle." As we will see, being in this cycle is almost like entering a tall maze where options and choices seem to be fixed, limited, and not visible. Just as the physical tension of rage is a central obstacle to be overcome in dealing with anger, so too is a cognitive form of tunnel vision a central obstacle in dealing with the guilt cycle. That is, people seem to respond cognitively to unacceptable demands as if they have been deprived of the ability to consider alternative responses, as if the only two choices available to them seem to be either to press on into darkness or to go back. Those caught in guilt often see equally poor choices. As we trace the guilt cycle and view its development, the "tunnel problem" will become clearer.

How do we react to unacceptable or unrealistic demands? Actually, the first response is usually surprise. If we could hear our inner response to such demands, it might be "You want *what*?" Once the initial surprise of an extraordinary request has passed, we are prone to feel annoyance or anger, depending on the degree of unacceptability of the demand. Thus, if an old friend calls after several years of no contact and asks to move in for six months, it is not uncommon to feel annoyed, if not angry, and say internally, "You must be kidding to place such an extreme burden on me." If the demand feels totally unrealistic (let's say you live in a two-bedroom apartment with six children) or unacceptable (e.g., your friend is known to be a freeloader who wanders around the country imposing on anyone he can), it is anger that is evoked in this part of the cycle. Somewhere inside us a voice may say, "My goodness, what nerve!"

He Who Is Passive Is Lost

Following surprise and annoyance or anger, there is a behavior that does the most to produce guilt. This stage can be described as passivity, which may come in at least two basic forms: passive compliance or simply doing nothing. We either give in, despite our hesitancy, to the demand or do nothing and hope that the person making the demand, or the demand itself, will go away. Either form of passivity creates the fertile ground for guilt. When we conform to or comply with demands that are contrary to our standards, we have let ourselves down and feel guilty. And when we do nothing, the absence of any meaningful response leaves a vacuum that is often experienced as guilt.

Passivity does accomplish something—it provides temporary relief. Once we have given in or the other person realizes that we plan to do nothing, the crisis and tension created by the excessive demand pass. Temporary relief gives us time to relax and to proceed to the next step, which is usually reflection. Few of us are so callous to ourselves or to others as to let the compliance or nonresponsiveness pass unnoticed. Gestalt psychology tells us that unfinished tasks are the ones we remember best. Passivity leaves a void or incompleteness; it leaves either a hole in our personal integrity from allowing someone to bully us into doing something we objected to or a hole in our self-image because we let someone down. Reflection on the passive behavior usually results in guilt, that gnawing feeling that we let ourselves or another down. Something is unfinished, something is still "owed." The diagram below illustrates the cycle that guilt tends to follow.

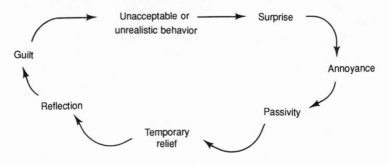

Creative Responses to "Crazy" Demands

When faced with another's demand, we need not feel we must passively comply or do nothing. Instead, we can decide what it is we desire to offer and make that offer genuinely. What this means is that when we are faced with the demands of others, we must learn to separate the person from the request. Once that is done, we are no longer stuck with saying either yes or no. Instead, we may ignore the unacceptable demand and focus on a personally desired response to the person. In this way, the tunnel vision produced by an unreasonable or unacceptable demand is broadened. Without the constraint of the demand, we can now ask useful questions: "Do I care about this person?" and, more important, "What is it I care to do for this person?" or "Is there anything I wish to do in response to this person's state of need? How do I truly desire to respond?" For example, suppose an old acquaintance calls and tells you that he is in debt and needs $10,000. The reflexive response would be to feel that giving the money or saying no were the only two alternatives. But another approach would be to ask "What do I care to do about this person?" Freed from the trap of yes or no, you might consider what you would be willing to do; for example, you could offer a lesser amount, introduce him to a wealthy generous friend, help him find a part-time job, babysit so his wife can work part time, and so on. The point is that in choosing your desired way to help you can respond freely. Granted, the person making the demand may not be as happy with your offer as he would be with compliance. However, since your offer was made after a careful attempt to respond in earnest and with your personal best, you are likely to feel better. Besides, who says you alone must resolve his entire problem? Since you have made a genuine response, any remaining guilt will be less burdensome. In fact, if the other insists that the only way to meet his demand is in his prescribed manner, it is he who has a problem.

To further illustrate the meaning of this personal and creative response to guilt, I offer the following story, told to me by a survivor of the Holocaust. The event took place in the Auschwitz concentration camp during the period between Rosh Hashana, the Jewish New Year, and Yom Kippur, the Day of Atonement.

In one barracks there was a group of Jews, some of whom were observant and some who were not. They were discussing the coming of Yom Kippur and struggling with the fact that tradition prescribes "repentance, prayer, and charity" as virtues that a Jew must aspire to in order to effect the forgiveness sought on Yom Kippur. Their struggle on that fall day centered on the impossibility of giving charity. How could one give charity in Auschwitz? Who had money? Who had presents? What on earth was there to give?

As these earnest soul searchers struggled for an answer, one began to cry. As he did, he lifted his battered tin ration cup to his eyes and several tears fell into the cup. This cup of tears was then passed from one inmate to another. This story poignantly illustrates that people can create solutions when they look for an inner genuine response.

What emerges from our discussion in this chapter is that feelings are not as plain as they may appear. Tension, anger, sadness, and guilt are, in their own ways, complex pieces of emotional machinery. It is when the separate and distinct gears of this machinery are seen and understood that these feelings become more manageable. This understanding becomes the starting point from which couples can learn to respond more humanely and effectively to each other's feelings. In this way seemingly irrational emotions can be used to see and paint a more understanding picture of the relationship. Learning to blend these colors is a process that demands patience. Often, only after repeated and patient attempts by trial and error do more satisfying results emerge. The commitment to try and to struggle is ultimately what shapes us all into being more competent artists in our pursuit of mutual understanding.

The art of understanding will be addressed in the chapter that follows. Particular attention will be paid to the art of self-understanding and self-care.

Chapter 6

SELF-MAINTENANCE

You can't change the music of your soul.
—Katharine Hepburn

Therapist: Why did you get married?
Arthur: Loneliness, I suppose.
Therapist: Didn't you have any friends?
Arthur: I've always had some friends.
Therapist: What more were you looking for?
Arthur: I guess I got tired of taking care of myself. It's scary. I
 wanted someone to help.

While loneliness and the need for companionship are popular reasons for people to form relationships, the desire to have someone
fill in our personal gaps is perhaps equally as common. Some people
are frank enough to say that they hoped their spouse would complement them: "I'm impulsive, he's conservative"; "I'm more passive, she's better with decisions." Certainly, some relationships find
a mutually satisfying complementary balance. In others, however,

79

one-half plus one-half does not make a whole; instead, it makes a quarter.

A common phrase heard by marital therapists is "I'm not getting what I want." Some people will battle, argue, and cajole to try to get the other to meet their needs. Even if lack of ability, illness, or sheer stubbornness makes one partner unable to meet the other's needs, the needy one will keep thrashing away until they both hate each other entirely or are exhausted.

One of the most peculiar experiences I have as a therapist comes when I ask people to make a list of ten things they can do by themselves, for themselves, to make themselves feel happy. Few people get beyond listing five items. Others look stupefied. For some, it takes days to distinguish between what they can do for themselves and what others can do for them. Surprisingly, many have little or no idea what their needs are.

KNOWING YOUR EMOTIONAL NEEDS

Self-maintenance, that is, pulling your own emotional weight in a relationship, is a key factor in keeping relationships going. However, if you are to pull your own emotional weight in your relationship, it is essential that you be able to identify your needs—a task, as we have noted, that is not easily done.

Broadly speaking, needs come in two kinds: independent ones, which we can fill by ourselves, and dependent ones, for which we must rely on others. The first step toward self-maintenance is to learn to distinguish between independent and dependent needs. Many of my clients have difficulty with self-maintenance because they confuse needs they can fulfill independently with those for which they need others to provide gratification.

The ability to tell dependent needs from independent ones can have important benefits, including (1) increased potential for self-respect, (2) possible gains in self-confidence, and (3) decreased friction with one's partner. We each have, and need to have, both independent and dependent needs; how we manage them can mean the difference between joy and despair.

People sometimes confuse identifying and meeting one's own needs with the kind of selfishness often called "doing my own thing." Assuming responsibility and taking charge of one's own needs is a method of self-sustenance rather than self-exclusion. It is a way of making oneself whole, so that instead of multiplying one-half by one-half when one person meets another, what emerges is more than a fraction. Once one is in a position of familiarity and fluency with one's personal needs and is accomplished at meeting them, relationships can be less of a risk. As a client in one of my group therapy sessions once said, "I would like to get to the point where I want to be with people, instead of feeling like I need to be around them."

INDEPENDENT VERSUS DEPENDENT EMOTIONAL NEEDS

What, then, does it take for people to take charge of their own needs? First, they need to stop waiting and expecting someone else to do the job. All the people I know, in some way and in some area in their lives, are looking for someone to take care of them. Self-maintenance requires letting go of the illusion that it is someone else's job to take charge of your needs. It also means examining which of your life needs can be handled independently and which can be safely entrusted to others.

This distinction between independent and dependent needs is also useful in understanding periods of personal unrest. This point is illustrated by the story of Alex, a client who was experiencing considerable pain. When Alex came into therapy his life felt unmanageable. He had waited until his late thirties to get married because he was afraid of repeating his parents' pattern of early marriage and divorce. After less than a year into his marriage, Alex found himself looking at other women. Such behavior surprised and disturbed him deeply.

What emerged from Alex's hard work in treatment was that he had always experienced periodic depressions and restlessness. In order to get out of these "ruts," Alex changed jobs. He had even moved to a different city on several occasions. Now married, Alex was again feeling restless, depressed, and trapped. Somehow, however, he knew that seeking a relationship outside the marriage was not what he really wanted.

In a group session one night Alex finally put his problem this way: "I guess I have two kinds of needs: me needs and other needs. When I'm bored, I'm never sure whether I need to do something for myself or whether I want someone else to make me feel better." It seems that Alex would confuse these two types of needs, which would usually lead to disaster. Looking to others or pressuring them for love would make Alex feel even more empty and cynical about relationships.

In the end, Alex discovered that "me needs" were those relating to personal gaps. His periods of restlessness revealed themselves to be the result of a need for personal achievement. Alex had taken jobs in areas below his skill level; he had a good mind but had been afraid to apply himself in a disciplined school environment. When Alex began focusing on this particular personal gap, his restlessness eased. He learned that trying to fill "me needs" by relying on others was an error; he learned to fill his own cup instead of asking others to do something only he could do for himself.

EMOTIONAL SELF-CARE: SOME FIRST STEPS

You can start the process of self-maintenance by listing your needs on a sheet of paper. Next, divide another sheet into two columns under the headings Independent Needs and Dependent Needs. Once this division is made and your needs are on paper, you are ready to see what kind of job you are doing in taking care of yourself. Look first at the column of independent needs. How well are you meeting those needs? How consistently do you take care of them? How well do you work on them when you are hurting or feeling down? The answers to these questions will give you an initial reading. Next, see how many of your needs are in the column marked Dependent Needs. If most of your needs are in that column, chances are that you are not taking very good care of yourself.

Here are some of the needs that my clients have identified:

- Need for physical well-being, including proper diet, exercise, and relaxation.
- Need for enjoyment of the world, including taking walks, looking at the stars, sunbathing, watching and listening to the surf, tasting snowflakes, and so forth.
- Need for caring, including the capacity to elicit and take in the affection of others.
- Need to give caring and affection, which involves the skill of being able to present what you want to give in a way that enables others to receive it.
- Need to set goals and pursue them; having dreams, short- and long-term plans to realize them, and a sense of purpose in life are common aspects of this category.
- Need for self-knowledge; many people seem to benefit from having some clarity about themselves, especially an awareness of their own strengths and weaknesses.
- Need for consistency, including both personal and inter-personal consistency; particularly important is having the sense that one's behaviors match one's feelings or some inner direction.
- Need for belonging or status in a select group, be it family, community, or a special organization.
- Need for fun, including diversions, hobbies, entertainment, and time for oneself.
- Need to be listened to and understood by another.
- Need for a higher power or for spiritual faith in God or simply in fate or luck.
- Need to touch and be touched by others, that is, physical contact with others.

- Need for financial autonomy or the securing of basic life services by earning money or via a reciprocal agreement.
- Need for intellectual stimulation, including time to think, daydream, read, or take classes.

This list of needs is in no way exhaustive; some of your needs may not be included here. What is important for self-maintenance is to have a fairly clear idea of what *you* need. Furthermore, taking on the task of identifying for yourself as many of your needs as possible will help you to take care of yourself. Clearly, if you cannot identify your own needs or feel you must rely on someone else to satisfy your needs, you are not in a good position to take care of yourself. While this need-identifying aspect of self-maintenance is difficult and may require a change in your thinking and behavior, once begun, it can become an adventure. You will find that you have needs you never knew were there and that those needs change over time. Most important, the benefits of this form of self-care begin as soon as you take even the smallest step. Self-maintenance can feel joyful and vitalizing. When pursued in the context of a strained relationship of any kind, it takes pressure off the relationship. Once your partner feels you are taking more responsibility for meeting your needs, the pressure on him or her is eased. This then may allow your partner to more freely consider what more he or she needs to be giving you.

THE HAZARDS OF SELFLESSNESS

Howard is the kind of man who has always had problems expressing his needs. Howard's father died when Howard was ten years old. After his father's sudden death Howard saw himself as the "man of the house." Although he shared responsibilities with his younger brother and sister, Howard clearly felt that the burden lay on his shoulders. He felt that this perception of his role was supported by those around him: his mother would stress how much she needed his help, and when his priest or some of his dad's friends would ask him how his mom was getting along, Howard figured they were asking whether he was doing a good job.

Howard's perception of himself as a man was further developed by his social experiences. The most valued trait among Howard's friends was "being able to handle yourself." Modeled after movie heroes like John Wayne, this attitude meant that a "real man" was both independent and self-sufficient. In short, Howard's attitude was that in order to be proud of himself and earn the respect of others, it was essential that he need nothing from anyone.

Not surprisingly, Howard became a caretaker sort of person: he was most comfortable taking care of others. As the big brother and "mother's little man," he was both protector of the family and master of errands. Howard learned to become resourceful. As he ran errands, he learned about shopping for quality goods and how people did business. When it came to home repairs, he never asked for guidance or help, learning largely by trial and error or from watching the carpenters and handymen, who were so plentiful in his neighborhood, and then copying what he saw.

Lisa met Howard in high school. He was the only boy she knew who was what she called a "serious person." She was attracted to Howard's capacity to plan. Whether it was building the stage scenery for a school play or getting to a rally downtown, Howard always seemed to know how to get things done. What's more, Howard already had a job and plans for the money he was earning.

According to plan, Howard and Lisa married shortly after their second year of college. They were able to afford a nice apartment and lived happily enough. At this point Howard was going to school full time to obtain a degree in business. He also held a part-time job for an accounting firm and his old Sunday job as a waiter and took on any odd jobs he could pick up.

Lisa was proud of Howard. Her own father had been an uninspired clerk at the State Department of Motor Vehicles. Lisa had suffered through years of quarrels between her mother and father that centered on his apparent failure to "make something of himself." In contrast, Howard was a breath of fresh air. As Lisa's mother put it, "No grass will ever grow under that boy's feet."

Howard began to trip himself up when events occurred that were not part of his plan. Within a two-year period his mother took ill, his brother began college, and his sister became engaged. The financial burden generated by these events was more than anyone could have anticipated. As Howard scrambled harder to take care of these new and pressing needs, including generating plans to pay for a second tuition and a forthcoming wedding, he had trouble maintaining old plans for saving money toward a house.

For the first time since his father died, Howard felt at a loss. He would wake up in the middle of the night, careful not to wake Lisa, and calculate his income and projected expenses over and over again. He became fatigued, irritable, sullen, and, finally, depressed. He began to sleep late and miss classes and took to staring at the television for hours at a time. Lisa reacted to this change in Howard with panic. What has happened to my strong and capable husband? she wondered. Images of her own father haunted her thoughts. She pleaded with Howard to tell her what was wrong. Instead of telling her what was on his mind, Howard became uncharacteristically cold. He offered little more than to say, "Some problems have come up at work and I'll handle them. I just need time to figure out how." Internally, Howard not only felt inadequate because he had no plan to fix things, but also ashamed that his problems were affecting Lisa. Predictably, the more Lisa tried to help, the more emotionally tight, angry, and embarrassed Howard became. Surprisingly, the usually slender Howard gained nearly thirty pounds.

In therapy Howard began to confront his "weakness." He realized that his idea of his own needs was to be able to take care of everyone else. His younger brother was furious when he learned that Howard's depression was related to concerns about this second tuition; he had his own pride. Howard's sister was touched by her brother's caring. She and her fiancé decided to put off their wedding until they could better afford it and were comfortable asking his parents for more help.

Lisa had a terrible time in treatment. Feeling so helpless about the man she loved was a blow to her self-esteem. She certainly had some disappointment about the fall of her knight in shining armor, but more than that she felt hurt and angry about being so shut out. Lisa was furious that the therapist knew more about Howard's inner struggles than she did. When Howard admitted that he couldn't tell her that he had needed her encouragement, comfort, advice, and usually calming companionship for fear of looking incompetent, Lisa threatened to leave him. "Those are some of my best things to give," she warned. "Don't you ever block me from giving to you again." Howard was so shaken by this episode that he resolved to change.

The kind of change made by Howard illustrates how people can take personal responsibility for themselves. Howard had taken upon himself some emotional and financial burdens that finally overwhelmed him. As we worked in therapy, I asked Howard what his needs were, besides making the world right for everyone else! At first Howard interpreted this to mean that I, too, thought him inadequate. Later, he acknowledged that he had never given much thought to his needs; he considered such introspection to be selfish. In therapy Lisa was quick to point out to Howard that his behavior was the epitome of selfishness and irresponsibility. "You've been holding all the cards," she said. "You decided how many extra hours you would work. You decided how to allot the overtime funds you earned. You decided how much time you would be away from home. You even decided what information I could get about our problems! See, Howard, if that's not selfishness, it's plain totalitarianism! Besides, look at what this has done to both your physical and emotional health. You're slowly killing yourself."

Howard had some mixed feelings about Lisa's outburst. On the one hand, he felt she was an ingrate to criticize him so. He even felt some righteous indignation. After all, hadn't he done all this to protect her from being upset! On the other hand, when Lisa showed a loving interest in his needs and welfare, Howard felt honestly cared for. I encouraged Howard to go with his second set of feelings. I further challenged him to be more knowledgeable about needs he might have that were unrelated to Lisa. We decided that his having a commitment to discovering those needs would be a sign of personal strength and a way to make it easier for Lisa to show her love. As Lisa put it, "First of all, Howard, you will feel better about yourself if you can learn to make yourself happier. Secondly, that will make my job as a wife easier. I'd love to know more about what really makes you happy."

Being the planner that he is, Howard divided this new challenge of personal responsibility into three primary areas: physical needs, relationship needs, and spiritual needs. Howard methodically broke these three areas into smaller pieces, assigning each a goal. At first he was almost like a kid let loose in a candy store. More sleep, better diet, more recreation, more personal time all popped up in the physical realm. Howard set goals to get at least six hours of sleep a night and agreed to remain in bed if he woke up prematurely. Within a few weeks Howard began to sit down and have breakfast, something he had never done before. He also began to take a ten-minute daily break and found a place where he could learn to swim. These ways to take better physical care of himself became part of his weekly schedule.

Recontacting old friends to meet for dinner was how Howard began attending to some of his relationship needs. To have more time for themselves as a couple Lisa suggested that they commit themselves to eating dinner together on at least one weekday evening besides Friday night. They also agreed to spend at least a few moments simply holding each other whenever one or the other needed to be held.

Finally, Howard decided to get his spiritual life in order. For a long time he had been, he said, in a sort of "spiritual rut." He felt as if his relationship to God had become rote and routine. Although Howard had made it his practice to pray daily, his heart had not been in it for some time. Upon reflection and discussion in therapy, Howard realized that his spiritual life felt like a burden thrust upon him. His spirituality was actually divided into two parts that seemed to coexist but didn't interact. First, there was Howard's aesthetic side that stood in awe of the mountains he had once skied and marveled at the intricacy of the body's workings. Yet when Howard prayed or attended church classes, the awe for nature and love for the Creator of it all he felt never seemed to mix. As Howard began to appreciate the unique aspects of his relationship to God, he began to take responsibility for incorporating his aesthetic spirituality with what had become a ritualistic religious attitude. A particularly refreshing change from ritual took place when Howard would take any opportunity to study or pray outdoors.

NEEDS AND SELF-DISCOVERY

Some other aspects of self-maintenance are revealed by the experiences of a thirty-five-year-old client named Rose, who first came to see me after her divorce. At that time Rose had two main concerns: she was feeling ashamed of her divorce and she had begun to have panic attacks. At night, as it got dark, Rose's heart would begin to pound; she would put on the radio, call friends, or try to write poetry. No matter what she tried, she would get dizzy and fearful that she was going to faint or die alone in her apartment.

In treatment Rose revealed that she felt confused, having never had this kind of panic attack before. While she did not like the stigma she felt as a divorcée, she also was not lonesome for her exhusband. As we talked more, Rose was better able to distinguish between loneliness and feeling alone. Loneliness, to paraphrase psychologist Carl Jung, is a state wherein you are unable to say the important things about yourself to someone who matters. Rose had good friends who mattered to her and who cared about her. If she felt lonely it was her own fault, because she merely had to let her friends know she wanted company and they were glad to be there for her.

Feeling alone or experiencing solitude was quite another matter. At first Rose denied that she had any problem with being alone; she fancied herself a rather independent person. Under closer examination we found that while Rose was an independent thinker and a self-motivated person, she had always surrounded herself with family, husband, or friends. Before her divorce being alone had never been a problem. On the contrary, in many ways, Rose had good balance between her individuality and social support. The divorce, however, had forced Rose into a new lifestyle: she was living alone for the first time. In addition, the divorce left Rose with a sense of personal failure and guilt. Estranged from her previous lifestyle and from her self-balance, Rose said she felt like she had been "put into exile."

When living alone was presented to Rose as a challenge instead of a punishment, she began to respond more effectively. She learned deep-muscle relaxation techniques to subdue the feelings of panic. Having come from a large family, Rose was unfamiliar with the experience of being alone. "There was always someone around," she explained. So at the age of thirty-five Rose began asking herself how best to care for herself when alone. Rose made some interesting changes that broadened her as a person. For instance, she noticed that flowers and music were especially soothing to her. Soon she took to keeping varieties of fresh-cut flowers. She even spent some of her alone time planning her own "porch garden." From listening to music for pleasure, Rose went on to learn to play the flute. Although she preferred times spent with friends, she began to learn to enjoy her solitary times. They became times of learning more about her private self.

DEPENDENT NEEDS AND THE CHALLENGES OF EMOTIONAL CONFLICT

Up to this point we have discussed how taking personal and independent responsibility for needs is an important aspect of self-maintenance. But, as mentioned earlier, there are also dependent needs, those that we cannot meet by ourselves but must rely on others to help us with.

How dependent needs are addressed can determine whether a relationship gets stronger or weaker. Many of the clinical examples so far have illustrated that when needs or feelings are met with shaming, blaming, or control tactics, the relationship can be seriously damaged. In contrast, when needs are identified and given attention, a strengthening of the couple's emotional bond occurs.

An examination of how dependent needs can be handled will help to explain what makes them such a powerful force. Too often, dealing with dependent needs in a marriage follows a pattern characterized by two stages: the conflict stage and the fighting stage. The conflict stage begins when one partner has a dependent need, that is, needs something from the other partner. When dependent needs surface, they usually do so in the form of an expectation. For example, one of the partners in a marriage may have a particular need to have his or her efforts acknowledged. This need for acknowledgment can be met when the other partner takes cognizance of the first partner's efforts and expresses recognition. Therefore, the first partner's need for acknowledgment is a dependent need. Once the expectation of acknowledgment has been verbalized, there are two possible consequences: (1) the needed praise will be received and the needy one will feel appreciated or (2) the expectation will not be met, resulting in disappointment and, ultimately, conflict.

Needs, expectations, and disappointments make up the conflict stage. When our needs are different, we are in conflict; at this point in the conflict stage neither partner has gotten hurt yet. If spouses can mention their feelings of disappointment, state their expectations, and articulate their needs, the conflict stage can most likely be resolved. Since disappointment is normally not a highly charged emotion, it can be lessened when expectations and needs are reevaluated.

Stage two, the fighting stage, is created when two people in a relationship do not let each other know that they are disappointed. With expressed disappointment there is a sense that expectations do not match what one receives; when the disappointment is unexpressed, it tends to fester until it becomes the emotion of hurt, which, if unchecked, can lead to anger. Again, retracing the steps described can resolve the emerging hurt. If people can say "I am hurt, you disappointed me; I had this expectation and this need," the feelings become more manageable and the needs more open to discussion. However, when hurt feelings are left unexpressed they turn into anger. Just as white corpuscles in the blood system serve to ward off infection, so too does anger, in our emotion system, serve to ward off longstanding or impending hurt.

Understanding Anger: Turning Trouble into Tranquility

Anger, too, can be resolved by reversing the steps that lead to it, namely, hurt, disappointment, expectations, and needs. Couples tend to fight the hardest, and for the longest lengths of time, when they are stuck in the anger step and are unable or unwilling to address their mutual hurts. In the event that anger is also left unstated, it moves into depression.

One of Sigmund Freud's[8] most useful insights was his understanding that anger can turn into depression. Thus, in a relationship where there is an overload of angry feelings the partners may become depressed. This is most recognizable by long silences, little meaningful conversation, a decrease in overt affection, and lapses in sexual activity. Depression can be alleviated when the steps leading to it are retraced. This can be done by first calling attention to the hurt. There is no anger without hurt. Expressing hurt feelings changes the emotional tone. Whereas depression drains uneasiness or tension and anger usually evokes a defensive response or yet more anger, hurt elicits curiosity or sympathy. When someone tells us that he or she is hurt by our actions we wonder why or how. This openness makes looking at the disappointment and unmet expectations possible. These expectations and the needs they reflect are now ready to be explored. Both partners can now examine whether or how these needs might be addressed. Retracing the steps in this way will move the depressed dullness into the action and activity stage of question and response. The tension–depression is eased by asking several questions: (1) Did you know I was hurt?; (2) Do you understand my disappointment?; (3) Are my expectations clear?; and most important (4) Do my needs matter to you? Can they be met?

Apathy: The Silent Empty

Depressed relationships allowed to stay that way evolve into yet another aspect of the fighting stage: apathy. At this point people stop caring. After being hurt, angry, and depressed for so long, they seem to find some relief in giving up their caring. This psychological form of "cutting one's losses" brings with it a perverse, hypnotic kind of relief that comes from no longer caring. Statements like "It feels so good to stop beating my head against the wall" typically characterize the apathy stage. Unfortunately, apathy leaves people in a state of indecision. The only noticeable change becomes an increase in cynicism. Partners can still hurt each other, even though they stopped caring for each other long ago. The emotional bruises are still there, but the callus of apathy dulls the experience of pain. Time passes the couple by, and nothing changes.

Although relationships may remain in the emotional wasteland of apathy for years, they ultimately lapse into destructive behavior. Destructive behavior is the final phase of the fighting stage. After a time in a joyless relationship people get careless with themselves and their behavior toward each other. Addictions, extramarital affairs, separations, and, ultimately, divorce are typical of this phase. Despite the damage done by destructive behavior and apathy, the path to healing can still be undertaken when the couple decides to care enough to change. After mourning their losses and feeling the sadness that is so much a part of depression, couples on the way back to mutuality must pass through the now-familiar steps of anger, hurt, disappointment, expectations, and, ultimately, renegotiating needs. We now can see how much of the pain, tears, and anger in a relationship relates to dependent needs and the way they are expressed and responded to. The diagram below is offered so you can picture the course of conflict and the path to resolution just described. Note well that the arrows are reversible, to indicate the way back.

Needs ⟷ Expectations ⟷ Disappointment ⟷ Hurt ⟷

Anger ⟷ Depression ⟷ Apathy ⟷ Self-destructive (marital) behavior

SELF-ACCEPTANCE

An integral aspect of self-maintenance is "self-acceptance." Whatever level of self-acceptance that one may have is tried and tested during marital conflict. Experiencing the heat of a loved one's anger can easily mar one's self-acceptance. This can result in a desire to hide or cut oneself off from whatever has brought a loved one to be so displeased. In the search for compromise or an end to the anger, valuable parts of the self may be sacrificed. In times of conflict self-acceptance can be best maintained by thinking of oneself as a whole made up of several valuable parts.

You may have seen movies or cartoons in which heroes or bullies were shown as having two personalities or perhaps simply a good and bad conscience. Usually, the good and bad sides of the character are portrayed as antagonists or opposite extremes, one of which must win and take total control of the personality while the other, being defeated, is banished into oblivion.

This view is far from realistic. The multifaceted nature of man was vividly described to a client of mine by an army psychologist he consulted at a time in his life when he was undergoing battle-related stress. The psychologist, my client told me, listened to his fears and showed him a bucket of water. At first, the psychologist swirled the water into a foamy white bubbly turbulence. Later, when the water settled, he turned to my client and said, "You are like the water in the bucket. Both the turbulence and calm are you; one is as much a part of you as the other."

ATTITUDE AND SELF-CARE: APPRECIATING YOUR WHOLE SELF

Seeing and treating oneself as a unified whole during periods of personal unrest is a vital part of self-maintenance. Each of us in our own way experiences times of turmoil, frustration, and conflict. The inevitability of painful aspects of living and the unpredictability of being human result in moments of personal exasperation. A common response to this is to feel fragmented or angry or unaccepting of oneself as a whole or of a facet of one's personality. Much the same way that people are prone to reject partners during relationship struggles, there is a tendency to reject aspects of ourselves when we are unhappy.

One of the most helpful things that I have ever learned was a comparison made by my grandfather, of blessed memory: he told me that every person is like a diamond and instructed me to look carefully in order to become aware of each person's unique beauty; people, like diamonds, are multifaceted and not easily comprehended. My experience as a psychotherapist has taught me that all aspects of a person's personality are in some way useful to them. Each characteristic or feeling has purpose and a potentially valuable place in the personality if the person is willing to accept each one and give it some expression. While life's difficulties create stress, it is when people reject parts of themselves that they usually create the most severe and lasting damage to their self-esteem.

Arthur was a person with low self-esteem. He felt unloved by others and lived in a state of ongoing guilt, which seemed to guarantee unhappiness. His mood was low and getting through most days was like drudgery. After a period of time in therapy it became clear to both of us that Arthur could take much better care of himself if he would allow himself expressions of anger or opposition. It seemed that these would help prevent him from being exploited by others and would diffuse his state of frustrated helplessness. There was, however, one obstacle: Arthur felt that being angry or oppositional was bad and dangerous. As a child, he would have temper tantrums that would leave his mother in tears. One day his parents took him out to the country and showed him an old, deserted house. They informed him that this was the place where people who were angry were kept. They warned him that he would be sent there if he continued his angry behavior. Arthur concluded that his feelings of anger were endangering his life and promised his parents and himself never to show anger again. Arthur responded to this event in a way that shaped his entire life. What he learned was that a part of himself was dangerous and shameful. Until he could learn to use his anger to protect his unique gentleness, he remained withdrawn in interpersonal dealings. Without the knowledge that his anger could be both positive and useful, Arthur was emotionally stunted and unfulfilled.

While the manifestations and causes of personality fragmentation or denial of parts of the self are rarely as striking as in the case just described, the inability to appreciate one's whole self is a frequent and commonplace occurrence. Life offers its share of inescapable rejections and discouragements. Those of us who wish to maintain and care for ourselves can soften those blows by being careful not to do the same to aspects of our own person. A combination of curiosity, firmness, and gentleness about all aspects of the self, be they echoes of the tyrant, sadist, miser, fool, braggart, or wallflower, can provide a potent method of self-care. Rejecting those parts of the self can be as reckless as acting them out in a literal fashion.

It is important for self-care of this kind to be done with patience. Self-accusations and impatience in this work usually coincide with an unwillingness to take oneself seriously and an insistence that someone else do the work. Kindness to oneself can be of great help: a useful visual image may be to see ourselves as lifelong naive children who sometimes stray off into the daisies and who must be gently coaxed back onto the main road. Sometimes, as much as we may try to stay on the road to self-care, others in the family constellation of life events may bump us off that road. In the following chapter these diverting forces will be identified and examined.

Chapter 7

EMOTIONAL GAPS
AND INTRUDERS

Nature abhors a vacuum.

—Benedict Spinoza

In Chapter 3 we saw how couples can create considerable difficulty for themselves when they substitute control tactics for assuming personal responsibility. There are instances, however, when the control issue is not of the couple's own making. When parents, for example, are unsuccessful in bearing responsibility for their own happiness and fulfillment, a gap or vacuum is created that they may try to fill through overinvolvement in the lives of their children. If this overinvolvement or intrusion, commonly in the form of controlling behaviors that may or may not be conscious, is allowed to go unbridled, it can threaten the happiness of all concerned. Such was the case with Rachel and her mother, Eve.

UNFINISHED LIVES: PAVING THE PATH FOR INTRUSION

Eve was the youngest in a family of five, the only daughter. Her father was a brutish, coarse man who earned his meager living as a shoemaker. From youth, Eve was the smile he would not show. She would stand at the shop's counter, where she would greet customers, take their damaged shoes, return mended pairs, and collect the fees due. Customers preferred Eve's smiling presence to her father's brusque and unfriendly manner. As she grew older, Eve became a fixture in the shop. Her charm and cordiality made people feel at ease and, indeed, increased the popularity of the shop. She rarely left the shop except to go to school, but even then she felt guilty, knowing that since Mama was busy tending to the boys, Dad needed her to deal with the customers.

When Eve married, she chose an ambitious but self-absorbed man. Early in the marriage Eve was happy to be the wife of so charming a person as her Arthur; over time, though, she tired of being his valet. Arthur was a more pleasant man than Eve's father, and although he had a profession, he seemed to be swallowed up in his firm. His attention to Eve was slim and seemed to be forced.

When their daughter Rachel was born, Eve felt great pride. She also found a new, more satisfying mission in life: caring for Rachel was the most wonderful experience Eve had ever known. Almost from birth Rachel filled the growing gap in Eve's life. Arthur continued to be attentive only when Eve spent too much money or made decisions he did not like. In contrast, Rachel's innocent attachment made Eve feel as if she herself had been reborn.

For as long as Rachel could remember, she and her mother were almost inseparable. They played together, took walks, and, as soon as Rachel could speak, had long talks. When Rachel grew older, she was confused by the troubles her girlfriends were having with their mothers, for she and Eve were best friends. There was nothing they would not do for each other. This closeness seemed to please Arthur, who often bragged to his friends about his "two girls."

When Rachel met David, no one was more pleased than Eve. All her life she had prayed that her daughter would find a "good man." In Eve's eyes, David was both good and kind, although somewhat young. Both Eve and Arthur encouraged the young couple and were delighted when the two decided to marry.

At first, David did not mind the frequent phone calls his mother-in-law made to his wife. He liked her goodwill and her smile but could not understand why she and Rachel needed to speak so often. This confusion turned to irritation when Eve came along to pick out the young couple's furniture; David felt it was mother and daughter who made the selections.

Over time David's confusion and irritation became the source of arguments between him and Rachel. As the couple made decisions about insurance, automobiles, and home decoration, Eve was somehow always involved. As David became more annoyed, Rachel felt more hurt. "Why," she would ask, "must you begrudge my mother the pleasure of helping us decide?" As David became convinced that Eve was a problem, Rachel became more nervous and depressed.

Finally, after several arguments about Eve's frequent calls and "suggestions" to the young couple, David angrily accused Rachel of being immature. Rachel felt torn but promised David that she would try to act more independently. Yet whenever the couple tried to leave Eve out, Rachel would feel upset, guilty, and worried. Increasingly, Eve would make efforts to "help out," such as paying for things or calling someone who could give the couple advice. When David lost his temper and told Eve to stay out of their lives, matters became worse. Eve would call Rachel, asking her what she had done wrong; Eve seemed to be in a panic. Then she would stop calling for weeks, only to resume the intrusive behavior pattern. Rachel felt trapped: she could neither bear David's angry accusations of immaturity nor stand to watch her mother's sadness and fear.

The unhappiness experienced by Rachel and Eve is typical of the anguish that occurs when personal responsibility gaps and the need to control combine. The emotional gap in Eve's life existed long before Rachel came along. From the early days of her own childhood, Eve had learned little about taking responsibility for her own happiness. She had always been an extension of her father—and later of Arthur. Her role in both relationships had been to meet the needs of the other. This pattern was repeated again in Eve's rearing of Rachel. When David pulled Rachel away, Eve's emotional gap broadened, as did her desperation to keep Rachel close. A renewed rash of phone calls and unsolicited advice was Eve's way of clinging to some control.

In therapy when David spoke of his anger with Rachel and his mother-in-law, he faced a dilemma. How could he continue to make his own decisions and feel like an adult with Eve's regular intrusions? On the other hand, how could he be so coldhearted as to break up the closeness that existed between these two women? Furthermore, what was he to do about his growing feelings of disdain for Rachel? He had always felt proud of her energy and enthusiasm, but seeing her react to her mother's moods and give in to what he called her "emotional blackmail" had diminished the respect David felt for his bride.

Eve, too, was perplexed and upset. She did not understand David's charges that she was meddling. "How could anyone take my caring for them to be meddling?" Eve asked herself. As she saw David's anger in action, her concerns grew. She was frightened by the intensity of the anger she saw and worried about Rachel. Eve felt that to stop calling Rachel would be letting her daughter down at a time when she needed a friend, yet to call as often as she liked seemed to fuel the fire of David's anger. In the end Eve's concern for Rachel won out over her fear of David's anger. She began calling even more often. When her intrusions, both by phone and in person, ignited arguments between the couple, Eve would try to settle the disputes in much the way she had calmed dissatisfied customers in her father's shop. This enraged David even further and deepened Rachel's feelings of being trapped and torn.

Remaining the emotional center of her mother's life had left Rachel a little girl who could not meet the demands of married life. Separating from her mother made her feel disloyal and awful, but because of his anger David did not seem to be an appealing alternative. Trying to fill the gaps in her mother's life nearly cost Rachel her marriage and her sanity.

In the end Rachel was able to regard herself as an individual with a responsibility for leading her own life. Therapy enabled Rachel to restore her vision of herself. She relinquished dreams that made unreasonable expectations and embraced those that vitalized her life. As Rachel let go of those expectations that she inherited from the debris of her mother's unfinished life, her own unique needs came into better focus. Having a clearer vision of her own agenda made it easier for Rachel to say no to more of David's wishes and yes to his actual needs. As David emerged from the morass of frozen shame and anger he, in turn, was better able to tell Rachel more of what he really needed from her. He learned to give Rachel more time and support to develop her creative talents. David finally learned to stay close to Rachel without giving in to the compulsion to fix whatever was bothering her. This last piece was especially liberating for Rachel, who now felt less burdened by the expectation that she lead a life already chosen for her by David or her mother.

THE SAD SWITCH: CHILDREN WHO LIVE THEIR PARENTS' LIVES

We can see that in this world of gaps between need and reality it is hard to tell who the adults are. Eve clearly is a parent yet at times she seems to be a frightened and dependent child. Rachel is a child who seems to be responsible for Eve's happiness; she feels the same worry that a mother might feel about a helpless child. Allow me to share yet another example about emotional gaps.

Barry's struggle with self-esteem, shame, and failure provides another example of how emotional gaps in a family affect the lives of its members. Barry's story actually begins before he was born. Arnold, Barry's father, was the oldest and brightest child in his family. Although no one in Arnold's family had ever attended college, it was the family consensus that Arnold would go to college and study to become a physician. Life circumstances—both the Great Depression of the 1930s and Arnold's meeting Hilda—interfered with the family's prediction. During the depression years, Arnold's family struggled to keep everyone housed and fed, and plans for Arnold's higher education were abandoned. Everyone was needed to work and contribute to the family's welfare. Arnold dutifully filled his role as the oldest and worked long hours; his dreams of a medical career faded as the economic pressures mounted. At the same time, Arnold met Hilda, another working teenager. They fell in love and were married. Barry was born a year later. By the time the effects of the depression had subsided, Arnold had acquired new responsibilities of his own: he now had a family to support. Dreams of college were sacrificed for making a living. Arnold never recovered from the gap between the physician he dreamed he could be and the carpet salesman he was. This gap, and the sense of loss it carried with it, made Arnold an unhappy, critical man who downgraded others in a desperate attempt to protect his damaged self-regard. Both Arnold's unhappiness about his personal gap and his style of criticism were to have a powerful and negative effect on Barry.

For a long time, Barry and his father were emotionally close. They confided in each other and generally spent considerable time together. It was during these confiding talks that Barry learned of his father's disappointments. A loyal and adoring Barry anticipated his father's wishes: he set out to be the physician his father had failed to become. At first, all went well. Barry was gifted with some of his father's intelligence; he had also inherited some of his father's early intellectual curiosity and enthusiasm for learning. Arnold delighted in Barry's capabilities. He carefully encouraged Barry's ambitions and directed them with criticism when Barry strayed off course.

Finally, the efforts of father and son bore fruit when Barry was admitted to medical school. Both were excited and filled with joy. Barry worked diligently and with a sense of purpose; he loved the natural sciences and did well in the critical first two years of school. But during his fourth year Barry began to have trouble. His grades for clerkship courses, where he was asked to deal with actual hospital patients, were not good. Barry would freeze in the clinic; he was unable to perform the procedures he had learned and understood. After several occurrences of these "freezing-up" episodes, Barry was referred for a psychological interview.

In the office it became clear that Barry was a terrified and depressed young man. He had such difficulty that he had to withdraw from school for several semesters. During this period his relationship with his father became seriously strained. Arnold felt that Barry was copping out and letting him down. He was openly critical and hostile to Barry and the psychologist.

Months of therapy revealed that Barry had become trapped in a cycle of low self-esteem, shame, and a sometimes overwhelming fear of failure. Many of these issues surfaced for Barry at the very beginning of his clinical clerkships. Barry loved science and problem solving, but he was terribly uncomfortable touching or physically affecting people. This realization caught him by surprise: he had always believed that he would like helping the sick. As it turned out, Barry didn't want to directly deal with sick people. What's more, Barry was certain that what he did want was to do medical research; several areas of endocrinology and neurology fascinated and excited him. Forcing himself to practice hospital medicine because he was unable to face his father's disappointment, caused Barry to freeze up in emotional paralysis.

Barry was not a simple conformist. As mentioned, he acquired strong feelings of his own about neuroendocrine research. Yet he felt that pursuing and fulfilling this inner drive would make him a failure in his father's eyes. "What kind of money are you going to make in research?" was Arnold's reply to Barry's explanations. "All you are going to do is waste a lot of time puttering around some lab, when there are people out there in real pain," added Arnold. His father's displeasure left Barry feeling ashamed of his own lifestyle choices. Months would pass before the creative young researcher could feel anything but shame and unworthiness. In short, since he had left his father's dream unfilled, Barry was paying dearly.

THE IMPORTANCE OF SEPARATION
AND INDIVIDUATION

Psychologists believe that one way such unhealthy ties to parents as Barry's can be prevented is through successful negotiation of the developmental task called separation and individuation, in which the child changes from a largely dependent to an autonomous individual. This shift is not merely one of leaving behind the physical and financial dependence of a child, for it also involves a critical shift in perspective. Individuals must shift from seeing others as responsible for their welfare to viewing themselves as master of their own needs and destiny. It is interesting to note that the passage in Genesis reads that a man first "leaves his mother and father"; it is only then that he may truly "cling" to his wife and, with her, finally form an adult unit. Thus, it was only when Rachel's mother, Eve, began to take charge of her life and mourn the childhood she herself had missed that she was more fully able to enjoy her life and allow Rachel to separate from her and become truly autonomous. When Eve began to attend to her own gaps, Rachel was better able to relate to her as a mother, instead of as her own child, and to continue her own development toward full adulthood.

Relating to parents or other family members who do not attend to their own gaps or needs can severely try a relationship. However, it is important not to give up on a spouse who is enmeshed and trapped as Rachel was. Such people have a deep sense of loyalty; helping them or waiting for them to get "unstuck" can be well worth the wait. Yet one cannot simply tear enmeshed people apart from each other, as David learned.

What does help those caught in this situation is the adoption of an attitude of calm solicitude, as if one were trying to guide a blind person through a minefield. Patience and learning to give calm caution are especially helpful. When one's spouse gets trapped by the emotional needs of parents, siblings, friends, or even one's own children, he or she may develop what I call the "Charlie the Tuna syndrome," named after the cartoon fish used in a TV commercial to sell a brand of tuna fish. In the commercials Charlie is always trying to do something that he hopes will satisfy the tuna canning company. Try as he may, he somehow always falls short and is told, "Sorry, Charlie." Somehow in spite of his efforts to please, he never has exactly what it is that the company desires.

People who get enmeshed trying to fill the gaps in the lives of those who intrude upon theirs continually offer their best efforts. With each new distress the intruders express their hopes: "If you will only do this for me, all will be better." Again and again, our own Charlie the Tunas do their best, only to hear "Sorry, it didn't work. I'm in trouble again."

Being "hooked" repeatedly, these enmeshed spouses lose confidence and self-esteem; they may even become unknowingly angry. Yet pride, stubbornness, fear, or mere habit keeps them trying to fill those gaps. Often, being a good coach can make the difference between exasperation and peace. Coaching in the familiar Lamaze method of childbirth requires that the father patiently remind the laboring mother of the stages of childbirth; he gives encouragement to help her focus on breathing properly. Similarly, enmeshed spouses need coaching, reminding, and encouragement. They need a kind of coaching that provides an active awareness of their emotional strengths and weaknesses. Remind them that expectations of themselves, in regard to their families, must take these strengths and weaknesses into account. Helping them to maintain a balance between what is expected and what they can honestly provide is crucial. This balance is particularly important as it relates to how emotional energy needs to be exerted or conserved. Further, they need encouragement to do what they can and to avoid being overly discouraged by what they cannot do.

Showing love to those who have gaps is a vital part of family life. However, if they continue to give without limits they themselves will be depleted. Repeatedly and lovingly, enmeshed spouses need to be made aware that, no matter what they do, their ability to fill gaps in the lives of loved ones is a nasty illusion.

Everyone has gaps; being limited is basic to being human. Accepting what cannot be helped and trying hard to change what can be is a choice. However, choosing to be bound to intruders, continuing to attempt to fill gaps whose completion must inevitably defy our efforts, can have ruinous consequences.

"EVERYTHING FOR THE CHILDREN": A RUINOUS REFRAIN

Young couples often do to their own children what their parents did to them. Young parents, who were themselves "gap-fillers" for their own parents, tend to recreate situations in their own lives in which they become emotionally dependent on their own children. This phenomenon is most easily seen in situations where children become more important members of the family than the parents who brought them into the world. There are special times when children's needs have priority over those of their parents. Because of their helplessness, the needs of infants deserve such priority if they are to survive. If and when parents are insufficiently prepared to give the infant's needs top priority, the infant is vulnerable to a variety of developmental problems.

Times of crisis, including severe illness and academic or social failure, also require that a child's needs be given temporary priority. During these times the entire family may need to make a priority shift to deal with the crisis. However, in many families, the priority given to a newborn child is never reversed. Instead, one or both parents continue to maintain the child's needs at the highest level of priority, long past the time when such special attention is necessary.

When parents' obligations to themselves are continually overshadowed by attending to the children, an emotional rift between the couple is unavoidable. Even when both parents agree to place their relationship in a subordinate position to the needs of a child, the results are usually unfavorable. Giving children top priority makes them intrusive to the parents' original relationship. This is even more true when one parent changes focus and priority to a disproportionate degree than the other. Openly or covertly, the parents will need to mourn this shift. Mourning is a necessary part of accommodation to change, and it includes a stage of anger. If the parents allow the shift to be anything more than temporary or the imbalance remains unchanged, that anger can easily be subversive and splinter the couple. Sadly, couples who are unable to resolve this mourning, change gears, and make this shift find that their previous level of intimacy is lost. In its place is the anger of one partner who feels left out and a void in the relationship that is created by the other partner, who is evidently living only for their child.

People seem to have an inner drive to live their own lives as completely as possible. When the responsibility for that personal fulfillment is shirked in favor of the children, a double danger emerges: first, the adult is left with a lingering sense of failure and the resulting low self-esteem or emotional shame and, second, someone else within the family system must take on the responsibility that has been shirked. As a result, one of the children will feel an obligation, either overtly or covertly, to complete the parent's unfinished desires or goals as if they were his or her own. Unfortunately for the child, this usually happens whether the child would freely choose such goals or not and irrespective of whether such goals are within the child's abilities or personal best interests.

When children become powerful enough to be an ongoing intrusion in their parents' relationship, it is likely to be a result of the parents' giving up on fulfilling their mutual contract or of one or both parents giving up on themselves. Children become intruders of serious concern when they have been prematurely graduated into being adult peers to their parents. Such children can be competitors to the marriage. This situation is bad for all concerned. If parents are able to keep their commitments to each other and to themselves, the usual minor intrusions that children present can be kept in perspective. When parents allow prolonged intrusions by a child, they lose the benefits of enjoying an adult relationship and children lose their chance to be children.

Intruders, to the extent that they endanger one's emotional survival, lose the right to be special. This is not to say that children need not do what they can for their parents or that parents ought not sacrifice for the benefit of future generations. It does mean that we—as both parents and children—have a responsibility to set limits when intrusion threatens our emotional health.

These dangers to emotional health were once illustrated to me by a mother and daughter who despite their considerable love for each other made each other miserable. Martha came from a broken home; members of her family suffered from low self-esteem and a lack of self-confidence. Martha avoided using her considerable business skills to realize a desired career and instead became bound to a hidden contract with her mother, Dora. The terms of the contract called for Martha to be the "best mother in the world" and to produce the psychologically sound and happy children her mother had failed to produce.

Martha was a hard worker. She worked overtime at making her daughter, Fran, as healthy as could be, giving her much care and attention. As the child grew up, both Martha and Dora rejoiced together in Fran's social and educational successes. Then it happened. Fran, who had not been in attendance to witness her mother's contract with her grandmother, began to show signs of stress: she began to have headaches and miss school. Suddenly her goals for her own profession became shaky and she broke off her engagement to be married. Fran then gave up her own apartment and moved back in with Martha. Fran seemed to need her mother's every moment to complain and share fears about her life. She expected Martha to give her full financial and ongoing emotional support. Martha found that she had no thoughts that were not filled with Fran's concerns and her own worries for her daughter. Martha was working extra hours at work to help provide for Fran's clothing and entertainment as well as being a full-time confidante. Finally Martha drew away from Fran, due to sheer exhaustion. When Fran became depressed, Martha attempted suicide and then entered therapy.

In the course of therapy Martha realized how emotionally dependent she had become on her daughter: her joys and disappointments were based solely on what Fran did or did not do. When

Martha began to realize and feel the extent of her dependence on Fran, she once said to me, "Sometimes, my daughter feels like a heavy growth."

When Martha was able to sever her tie to her daughter, two noticeable changes occurred. First, she and her husband drew closer, becoming friends and equal partners once more. Fran felt a tremendous relief; she felt she had endured the pressure of being an adult too long and decided to take a year off to be a child and play. Later, she entered a local art institute to fulfill her longtime secret goal to become an interior decorator.

Intrusions are costly. Whether they arise out of caring and concern or out of fear, they ruin relationships and rob people of their chance to exercise their own free will. Throwing out controlling intruders, however, must be done slowly, firmly, and gently, lest those involved suffer undue pain. For, as we have noted, intruders are usually people we are close to, people whose dreams and hopes for us are often not entirely different from those we need to develop on our own.

Chapter 8

THE COMPETITION CYCLE AND THE CRISIS OF TRUST: TWO MAIN CAUSES OF DIVORCE

People change and forget to tell each other.

—Lillian Hellman

In Chapter 3 we discussed how control erodes the positive attachment between couples. In addition to control there are two other
major enemies of marital intimacy that require careful examination:
the *competition syndrome* and the *crisis of trust.*

COMPETITION IN MARRIAGE:
AN ENEMY OF INTIMACY

In Western civilization competition has become the norm:
"getting there" first, financially and socially, is a national preoc-

cupation. Competition even extends to our methods of relaxation and recreation, that is, to sports and games. Marriages are especially vulnerable to the negative effect that competitiveness can bring. When couples meet and begin to know each other, they seem to have a way to accommodate each other's needs. There develops not only a give-and-take process but also a pace and rhythm. Perhaps it is infatuation that allows for such a free and fluid flow of emotional supplies! At some point in time, however, couples find that being there for one another is not as easy as it once was, that, in fact, it generates some friction. Inconvenience, fatigue, the intrusion of work and other demands on time seem to conspire to make meeting needs more difficult. Couples vary in their response to entering this newer, pressured, and unwelcome stage of their relationship. There are those who foresee the inevitable and plan out time for each other that can remain protected from these demands; others press ahead blindly, waiting for peace to return. Many partners seem to reflexively adopt the larger societal attitude and begin to compete with each other to get their needs met first. They may even thwart their partner from getting too far ahead.

A picture of how the competition cycle evolves can be seen through the eyes of Ann, the "terrorist." In appearance Ann hardly looked like a terrorist: she was pretty, with an innocent and pleasant smile. Her father was a minister of some reputation and a community leader. Although Ann's home was a busy one, ostensibly devoted to community service, she often felt like just another member of the "parish family."

Ann later married Mark, one of her university professors, and found him to be devoted to both her and his students. She rejoiced in Mark's sensitive attentions to her. Living in a university town with Mark was her dream of the quiet, devoted marriage. However, as her husband approached tenure, things began to change: Mark spent more time at the university, and he began to ask Ann to go to dinner with various members of the committees that he had recently joined. As Mark's ambition increased, Ann's importance to him seemed to decrease. It's not that Ann always needed to be on "center stage," but the feeling that she was just another member of the audience reopened old emotional wounds. The couple's special time alone seemed lost and displaced by Mark's new priority.

It was during the year that Mark became eligible for tenure that Ann's "terrorist activities" emerged. At first they seemed innocent enough: she would be late with Mark's dinner, which would make him late for his committee meetings. Occasionally, the usually reliable Ann would oversleep and forget to wake Mark in time for him to get to class. Later, the sabotage of Mark's pursuit of tenure became more damaging. Twice Ann came late to dinners with Mark's mentor, and once she, an experienced homemaker, ruined a dinner planned for Mark's colleagues. When Ann provoked a fight at the dean's reception, Mark had enough.

During treatment Ann spoke angrily about how Mark's career was frustrating her needs. "I didn't get married to be a showpiece and entertainer for strangers," she said. "I could have stayed in my father's house and done that!" Ann felt that Mark's needs for social visibility and acceptance were in competition with her needs for privacy and devoted mutual attention. Fearing that her needs were getting lost in Mark's pursuit of tenure, Ann felt she was going to lose the things most precious in her life. Thus, Ann the terrorist emerged in an attempt to keep Mark from meeting his goals; as Ann put it, "If I'm not going to get my dream, neither will he!"

Recognizing Signs of the Competition Cycle

This competing in the face of a reduction of available emotional supplies is a highly dangerous syndrome. At times in my practice it seems to be almost addictive. The partners each become so frantic to get their way that the spirit of being part of a loving relationship appears to evaporate.

The signs of the competition syndrome are pettiness, bickering, long arguments without resolution, and, ultimately, an attitude of "Why bother to talk about it?" As a couple escalates the competition over who wins, both the cooperation and the focus on needs that require attention get lost. What is left is the emptiness of asking

"Did I give in again or did I triumph?" The score is never even; each competitor sizes up the victories and losses and prepares to compete even more. One battle leads to another; with each battle more damage is done to hurt feelings and pride. Sadly, as time passes, it becomes more and more unclear what all the pain is about.

The harmful effects of this cycle are particularly apparent in the lives of Arnold and Nancy. Both were professionals and believers in high achievement. They met in graduate school, where they were both at the top of their class. After Arnold finished his degree in business, he became a regional director of sales for a computer software company. Although his job performance was excellent, he felt stymied at work. His boss never liked Arnold's aggressive style and passed over him twice to promote other employees. In spite of these repeated frustrations, Arnold drove himself and his staff harder so that his boss could not possibly pass over him a third time.

Nancy, too, was frustrated in reaching her goals. Although a corporate vice president at age thirty-five, she felt that she was fighting a losing battle to gain her father's respect. Her father, she felt, hardly noticed her accomplishments: his ear and affections seemed centered on Nancy's sister Shirley. As Arnold exhausted himself trying to satisfy his boss, Nancy exhausted herself trying to win her father's respect.

One of the consequences of Arnold and Nancy's frustration was that they were regularly out of sync with each other. Somehow, if Arnold came home feeling tired, Nancy was even more tired. On days when Nancy felt she needed a pep talk from Arnold, he, too, came home looking for emotional encouragement. As Nancy became more needy, so did Arnold. It even seemed that if one of them caught a cold, he or she would come home to find the other already bedridden! At first, the two of them would kid about how much alike they were. Later, they became cynical when they realized that the other was always more tired or depressed than they. As time passed, Nancy found herself fighting to get her feelings out before Arnold could complain about his day. Inevitably, each interrupted the other. They often felt as if they were playing the game Can You Top This Aggravation? Somehow, each lost the ability to care for the other. Life at home felt like a contest where both Nancy and Arnold felt like losers.

The greatest tragedy of the competition syndrome is the couple's gradual loss of their sense of positive attachment. Each begins, often without conscious awareness, to see the spouse differently. A shift in perception changes a once-loving best friend into a greedy adversary; in the end, two one-time cooperative companions become antagonists. The marriage ceases to be a source of solace and safety. Instead, it becomes a battleground.

As noted in the opening of this chapter, we live in a highly competitive society. The value placed on winning makes some of us competition addicts. That is to say, it is very difficult for some of us to turn down or back away from a challenge. Adults who competed with their siblings as children are most likely unaware of their tendency to compete. Men, particularly, from "expelling families" (see Chapter 2) are oftentimes blindly competitive.

This syndrome is insidious in that couples do not recognize the competitiveness. They may be aware of becoming increasingly frustrated and angry, but they rarely spot the competitive cycle on their own. Oddly, despite the tendency for the competitive syndrome to spiral, it can be quickly reversed. A reversal is made possible by two factors: a mutual willingness to stop the competition and the ability to define needs.

Winning against the Competition Cycle

Once the awareness and desire is there, the competition habit can be broken. What is required is a shift toward mutuality and cooperation. This attitude of mutuality is expressed in the Talmudic prescription that a husband ought to respect his wife as he does himself. The realization that competitiveness hurts the marriage team greatly improves the ability to change. Once it becomes clear that both partners must win in order for the marriage to flow more smoothly, a spirit of compromise and negotiation may set in. Rediscovering that they can complement each other and feel good about each other is often sufficiently reinforcing to couples to help them maintain the positive changes. Recurrences of the competition are likely, each time they are spotted and named they are more successfully and easily reversed.

Again, the ability to focus and be aware of one's own needs emerges as a critical skill for someone who is married. Breaking the competition syndrome requires that both partners identify what they want. Then they can ask for or negotiate for their needs rather than compete. Sometimes, people are conditioned to the business of competing without actually knowing what it is they want to receive if they win; for them, competing is an end in itself. The more precise we can be about our needs, that is, the more we can express them in terms of behaviors we want to appear or cease, the better non-competitors we become. As your partner's understanding of what will satisfy you increases, so do your chances of being able to enlist cooperation for what you want.

THE CENTRALITY OF TRUST

Trust is the foundation upon which all relationships are built. Without trust, all relationships ultimately fail. Having the simple faith that your partner will be fair, that he or she has your interests at heart, can help to overcome almost any conflict. However, once that trust erodes (or is suddenly destroyed), even the mildest struggle or mistake can cause the relationship to unravel beyond repair. The road to marital failure and divorce is steeper when prolonged bitter competition results in the loss of trust. When the competition syndrome accelerates to the point where a total adversarial relationship develops, trust can be lost forever. Once partners can no longer trust the other to forego a triumph or an opportunity to gain an upper hand, a critical stage has been reached.

Broken Trust

Loss of trust does more to destroy marriages than any other single cause. In my experience, couples can resolve the most radical differences as long as trust remains. In contrast, if trust has eroded owing to the prolonged effects of competing or has been destroyed by a sudden betrayal, even the simplest negotiations tend to end in failure. Trust can be ruined not only by competition but also when one partner breaks the primary rules.

Whether stated or not, most couples have a set of primary rules or agreements that form the basis for the relationship. Not surprisingly, primary rules are often needed to protect us from blaming, shaming, and intimidating. Examples of primary rules are "You will never hit me" and "You will never sleep away from home without explanation." Even the brutal sport of boxing is conducted according to clear regulations. Troubled marriages, too, need to have limits spelled out so that partners can once again trust that they will not be hurt indiscriminately. Typically, forbidden below-the-belt behavior may include raising family skeletons, citing past personal failures, making damaging comparisons to others, threatening to leave, or failing to inform the spouse of a night out. Whatever the basic rule, once it is broken a crisis of trust follows that shakes the relationship to the core. Some marriages simply end shortly after a breach of trust has occurred.

The troubles that befell Sue and Mike serve to illustrate the damaging effects of a crisis of trust. Sue and Mike had known each other since high school. Mike was an energetic and enthusiastic person. Sue was quiet, thoughtful, and cooperative. They had been friends for several years before getting married, with each serving as an adviser to the other. When Sue needed a push to apply to a better college, it was Mike who cheered her on. As Mike considered different business deals, Sue acted as the voice of caution. Friends saw Sue and Mike as a wonderful couple because they seemed to complement each other so well.

Trouble came shortly after Sue delivered their fifth child. Both Sue and Mike wanted a large family. What they had not anticipated were Mike's business difficulties. In spite of showing a knack for business in his youth, as an adult Mike came up short: he consistently managed an adequate income, but his "big deals" somehow always fell through.

Before their fifth child, Mike had taken his business failures philosophically. His attitude was simply "No risk, no gain." Time, fear, and failure, however, made Mike impatient. He had always dreamed of supporting Sue in grand style. Merely getting by had not been part of Mike's plan. Shortly after baby number five arrived, Mike took to investing large chunks of the couple's savings on the basis of various stock tips, engaging in questionable business deals, and even gambling.

When Sue first noticed the withdrawals from their savings account, she confronted Mike right away. Mike calmed her down and insisted that he would replace the withdrawn funds soon. When Sue discovered another savings withdrawal several months later, she was furious. She lectured Mike on the need to have savings for emergencies. Mike promised it would never happen again.

Meanwhile, in order to pacify Sue, Mike borrowed against a credit card and replaced half of the missing funds. Months later, interest payments for the loan had grown substantially. A speculative business deal had been Mike's hope to replace all the money and then some; when this deal failed, Mike was faced with goods he could not sell and even more debts. The combination of discovering Mike's deceit about the credit cards and his latest economic misadventures were too much for Sue. The broken promises and the financial state of emergency were more than she could bear. Sue insisted that Mike move out of the house and take his name off their checking account. Mike, for all his desperate efforts, felt emotionally abandoned. He felt that Sue had "pulled the plug" on him just when he needed her most. The two of them could hardly talk to each other. They were in the throes of a crisis of trust.

Repairing Broken Trust

Several steps can be taken to survive a crisis of trust. First, the behaviors that broke the trust must be identified. Next, both partners need to be clear about the fact that a basic rule was broken. Once the original ground rules of the relationship are verbally reaffirmed or modified, the couple has a basis on which to rebuild trust. Without this seemingly simple task of articulating just what is considered "below the belt," mistrust will likely increase.

Consistent adherence to safeguarding the established rules gradually allows for the other aspects of trust to be restored. That is, maintaining the need for honesty, consistency, and reliability will further cement the new bond of trust. Continued lying or dishonesty can easily uproot the delicate process of restoring trust. On the other hand, consistency in adhering to the rules does much to further trust. In fact, the more routine and predictable each spouse can be in following the new agreements, the more likely the crisis of trust will be overcome and mutual security will return. Repetition gives people a sense of reliability. Careful repetition without further deceit or excuse is an indication that both partners seriously desire a continuation of the relationship. These principles of trust restoration will be given more specific examination in the chapter on crisis.

Chapter 9

CRISIS

It is impossible to chase away the darkness with a stick.

—Rabbi Yosef Yitzchak of Lubavitch

Chapter 8 made reference to a specific type of crisis, which I labeled the crisis of trust. This chapter deals with the notion of crisis in general. A crisis is a period of extreme stress and tension; it is also an unavoidable reality of married life.

There are two sorts of crises that can put stress on a marriage: those that come from outside the marriage and those that originate from issues inherent in the relationship. Common crises related to external influence are family illnesses, deaths, sudden financial problems, and natural disasters. Those crises having origins in the relationship include a devastating argument, discovery of unfaithfulness, or an episode of physical abuse.

PEOPLE IN CRISIS: COMMON CHARACTERISTICS

Many couples find that when confronted with a crisis, they fall apart. Unfortunately, as children we are taught little about how to

handle crises—and less about what people in crisis are like. This
lack of information can result in critical misunderstandings in a
marriage. For example, when people are in a crisis, they undergo
changes: in order to cope with the strain and demand of a crisis,
they may become unusually pragmatic or selfish and often show a
temporary shift in values.

This "streamlining of personality," where people necessarily
narrow themselves in order to survive, can be confusing and upsetting to those around them. For example, we hear stories about
otherwise honest and principled people becoming dishonest and
stealing from others during times of panic or war. A soldier who
survived combat by thinking exclusively of himself and by strictly
following orders may return home to family and friends only to
find that he is accused of being selfish and unimaginative. It is
useful to understand crisis behavior so that couples can cope more
wisely when one or both of them is in crisis.

There are some things you should know about the effect a
crisis is likely to have on you and/or your partner. Whatever the
nature of the crisis, most people in crisis become increasingly self-
centered. To deal with a partner in crisis—be it a severe job problem, the onset of an illness, or a miscarriage—you will need to
understand that a partner's withdrawing from you and into the self
is a normal reaction. You need not take this behavior personally
by feeling left out or rejected. Furthermore, times of crisis are not
appropriate for dealing with long-range solutions or long-standing
relationship issues. The goal of contending with a crisis is to weather
it so that when the special pressures of the crisis are over, you and
your partner will have enough togetherness to work out any remaining issues.

DISTINGUISHING CRISIS FROM CONFLICT

One of the keys to managing a crisis is to discuss and decide
whether what has happened needs to be accepted at face value or
presents an issue in need of resolution. When a couple is in crisis,

they need to keep things simple, at least until the intensity of the crisis subsides. Again, the goal of dealing with a crisis is to survive it. The last thing a couple needs to do is to make a difficult situation worse by striking out at each other in reaction to the helplessness that a crisis brings. All too often couples react to powerlessness by intimidating or blaming each other simply to avoid the feeling of impotence that a sudden crisis like death or disaster can bring. Helplessness is hard to swallow, but scapegoating merely forces a couple to drink a mutual cup of poison.

EFFECTIVE CRISIS MANAGEMENT: KNOWING WHEN TO ENGAGE AND DISENGAGE

Dealing successfully (or as well as possible) with a crisis situation often depends on making the distinction between what can be controlled and what cannot. I've seen couples with a sick or dying child suffer added unnecessary damage because they were unable to accept that their crisis was a result of things that neither of them could control. It is difficult to be rational in a crisis, but one of the most harmful irrationalities is trying to pin blame on oneself or another when, in fact, no one has any real control over what has happened. Sometimes the best response that can be made to a crisis is to face the helplessness without recrimination.

Often, effective crisis management means literally getting more distance from your partner than you may be used to. The nature of the crisis may mean that your spouse will need more privacy to work through his or her feelings. If you are the partner in crisis, get used to asking for the "privacy" you need. If you are the one being asked to give space, remember that the reasons for more private space during a crisis usually imply no personal rejection: people in crisis simply need lots of time to think.

Emotional distance is also vital when a crisis is created by a heated argument. If you will recall what was said earlier about anger, there is a critical difference between "blowing off steam" and negotiating for change. In a heated argument couples often forget this vital distinction and undertake the impossible task of raging, blowing off steam, and negotiating all at the same time. When in crisis, try to allow yourself and your partner the privilege of being angry with what has happened. Release of the physical tension created by the crisis or the feelings it aroused is important, as long as this venting is not directed at anyone in particular. Yelling aloud or taking long walks are useful ways to relieve the physical tension of extreme anger or helplessness. Once the tension aspect of the crisis is eased, negotiating can then take place.

The process of how to negotiate has been explained in more detail in the chapter on communication (Chapter 4). However, when a big fight has generated a marital crisis, some added guidelines about negotiating may be useful:

1. Keep your early agenda to three key points or less. Remember that simplicity is essential. Focus on the present and minimize attention given to the past and the future.
2. Any time either you or your partner moves away from negotiating to blaming or blowing off steam, a time-out needs to be called. This time-out is geared toward allowing both of you to be sure that you have successfully dissipated whatever anger was in the way. Even though both partners have had turns at screaming or blaming and name-calling, one or the other may feel the need to do these again. Such behavior is to be expected. The idea is not to avoid these angry outbursts but to keep them separate from negotiating for changes, which is at the bottom of what the entire business was about in the first place.
3. Go slowly. Take extra care to determine that you both understand the proposals for change being offered. Make certain that your demands or concessions have been perceived as you intended. Be careful to clear up any aspects that seem vague. Failure to do so either out of naive trust, egocentric assumptions of perceived agreement, or cowardice will likely undermine all that you have been working for. An additional useful suggestion for many couples is to

list the feelings that are not appreciated and to write out the terms of the negotiation.

BASIC TRUST

Whether the source of a crisis has been some external event or some internal issue, the central element that seems to make a crisis difficult for couples is that it shakes one's basic sense of security. The feeling that one can give up some control to another without being hurt is at the heart of trust. In marriage this security should broaden to a capacity for mutual reliance; that each partner will act with the interests of the other in mind. As long as the basic trust between a couple is sustained, almost any threat can be met with some security. Once trust is lost, even the most minor unexpected problem can cause a major crisis.

Since it is so vital an aspect of relationships, trust is also vulnerable at times of crisis. When a disaster such as a family death, job loss, or illness occurs, a person's sense of security and trust is usually shaken. For example, you may find that after an in-law has died or been divorced, your spouse may seem less trusting and more suspicious of your love and loyalty. People sometimes misinterpret this natural response and consider it a threat, but a crisis invariably raises the questions "Who can I count on?" and "How much can I depend on them?" These are difficult questions for most people to answer, and it is usually those who are closest to the person in crisis who will be given the hardest time. This "testing out trust" is a necessary process and a normal response to crisis. When recognized as such, it is easier to respond with needed, clear, and concrete reassurances rather than the defensiveness that this practice of "testing out" sometimes elicits.

Trust is a more central problem when a crisis is produced by issues within the relationship. If you are caught in a lie, a sexual indiscretion, stealing, or physically abusive behavior, a loss of trust becomes the primary issue. Once trust is lost under these or similar circumstances, it is not easily regained. In the event that trust is lost, all else is secondary to rebuilding the trust.

The Process of Regaining Lost Trust

Here are some first aid procedures that can help couples experiencing a loss of trust. First, you will both need to clarify whether the trust that has been broken was based on an implicit or explicit agreement. Often, loss of trust is the result of one partner violating a rule or understanding that he or she did not know existed. Even when the rule is known, the importance it had for the other partner is sometimes underestimated or misunderstood.

Psychotherapists often hear an exchange between couples that goes something like this: "Well, what did you expect me to do, read your mind?" and, after a pause and some reflection, "Yes, I do; if you loved me, you would know what is really important." Reading minds is the gift of very few and, in my experience, not especially given to people simply because they love one another. Couples who want to relate need to be aware of the differences between explicit and implicit understandings. They also need to realize that if it is difficult to reach mutual agreement on explicit issues, then being in concert about unmentioned issues is harder by far. It is difficult enough not to disappoint another when each knows the rules; when the rules, for whatever reason, are not spelled out, violations are to be expected and should not be treated with bewilderment. Once you have gone through dealing with the hurt and anger, which always come with the breach of contract that loss of trust is, it is then crucial to focus on making the implicit explicit. Put your energies into clarifying whatever rules or expectations have not been clear up to this point. Discuss whether they are acceptable to both and come to an agreement, if you can, about future behavior.

If a trust has been broken, try to make an honest assessment as to whether you are really capable of following the expected rules. I have seen couples who, for one reason or another, make unrealistic or impossible rules or ones to which their partners are especially ill-suited. For example, I saw one couple who, because of their religious commitment, had an explicit rule that they would never get angry with each other and argue. They were bright, hard-working, achievement-oriented people whose sophisticated matrices of needs often collided, but they had agreed never to yell or fight. As a result, their relationship became so strained that one night they suddenly found themselves literally pounding on each other. After consultation with a rabbi and me, they found some way to work out their conflicting needs within limits that were more realistic for them.

We are all more or less aware that love is blind. Frankly, there is nothing wrong with love being blind. I'm sure many wonderful, unexpected joys result from this temporary blindness. However, when your vision returns and what you see in the clear light of day makes you less trusting of your partner, why suspect or blame him or her? Sure, they are not all that you hoped they would be—perhaps not even what *they* hoped to be for you. But who says that someone needs to be hurt further by the use of blame for coping with disappointment?

Once you and your partner have a more definite sense of what expectations you hold and have been explicit about which expectations can be realistically met, the renegotiation of trust can continue. Next, you will need to reestablish some ground rules. In cases where serious breaches of trust have occurred, I have observed that partners typically deal poorly with feelings of shock and hurt; they seem to react to lost trust by "hitting below the belt." This reaction of wanting to lash out creates particularly knotty consequences in that couples sometimes say the unspeakable: whether involving a black form of a pet name, a spiteful accusation, a carefully selected threat, or a well-chosen "emotional dagger," these attacks are especially damaging to the resumption of intimacy. In fact, unless the ground rules and boundaries are reestablished, future trust becomes impossible. The next step, then, is to clearly delineate which comments, comparisons, threats, and epithets are to be ruled as foul or below the belt.

Once these new boundaries and limits are renegotiated, both partners feel safer from the threat of being hurt, and the process of regaining trust may proceed. Next, some guidelines that describe trustworthy behavior need to be agreed upon. As we have noted before, nobody gets angry unless they want something to change. In a situation of lost trust, there are some limited and specific behavioral changes that will help rebuild trust, such as making that reassuring phone call, remembering to walk away when one is in rage, and being on time on that certain night. It is important that partners identify the behaviors that will help them feel safer and more trusting. Next, these guidelines need to be specified and, if possible, written down. When I work with a couple on restoring trust, we usually write down the identified behaviors and also which partner is responsible for which behaviors. I then date this makeshift contract, write a renegotiation date, and ask both partners to sign their names. Remarkably, few of these written agreements have ever been broken during the remaining course of therapy. Adherence to such an explicit agreement about trust-building behaviors seems to be a foundation stone to rebuilding lost trust.

There is a story told about the Ropshitzer Rebbe, of blessed memory, that bears on this point. The rebbe was once asked how the prayer of a zaddik (a spiritual leader) can change God's mind. He answered by quoting Rashi, a famous commentator on Genesis, who described the Creator as "building worlds and destroying them." When a zaddik prays, claimed the rebbe, he too builds a new world in which the "different decrees" of the "old world" do not exist. And it is a new world that couples must build to restore trust. The old world of broken promises and pain must cease, and in its place are new agreements, understandings, and behaviors that must now be safeguarded.

A word of advice regarding the choice of these behaviors: they must be clear, definite, and limited. The goal here is to construct a simple working agreement or contract. Though some partners prefer to try to gain a complete reworking of the relationship, this is usually neither wise nor possible. Keeping the number of trust-building behaviors small makes them easier to do and talk about.

Making them simple and clear (as opposed to statements like "Show me more love" or "Be more considerate") makes it easier for both partners to know exactly what is expected. Moreover, most people in a crisis are less able to perform complex tasks or meet complicated expectations. The greater the clarity with which these behaviors can be described and the easier they are to perform, the better the chances for managing this stage effectively.

SAMPLE CONTRACT

Jack will

- take more responsibility for the finances—pay the bills, balance the checkbook, make suggestions for budgeting—giving it as much time as it needs; consult with Jill
- help around the house, keep magazines off the floor, dump own and kids' clothes in the hamper, do dishes when he feels like it, take care of aquarium

Jill will

- make an effort give more compliments and be more supportive (e.g., say, "Thank you," "Good job," "I appreciated that," etc.)
- try to get things by making requests, rather than making demands

Both will

- call finance meetings when there is concern
- work at nonsexual hugs
- give reassurances

Signatures: ————————————— —————————————

Witnessed by: ————————————— —————————————

One of the most popular home remedies relied on by couples having a trust crisis is faith in the adage "Time heals all wounds."

Actually, time does seem to have some special healing powers in this area. Couples who have enough mutually satisfying ingredients in their relationship can rebound from a loss-of-trust crisis when given enough time. For some, the goodwill simply manages to outweigh the bad. For others, hope or optimism can solve the immediate hurt, and over time trust is regained. Yet there are times when neither of these factors alleviates the problem and time creates even more distance and a greater rift. When this happens, time needs to be given a direction and some help.

Two Healing Agents: Consistency and Accountability

In addition to the measures already discussed in this chapter, a combination of consistency and accountability offers a particularly powerful sort of help. Part of the reason why a loss of trust can be so destructive is that it creates a state of chaos in the relationship. At the heart of our desire for relationships is the promise of a sense of security or predictability. A steady relationship is a kind of emotional oasis in our busy and often stressful daily experience. Loss of trust attacks this real or imagined sense of security: what could be counted on before can no longer be taken for granted; what was once holy is now profane; what was once predictable is now uncertain. Thus, consistency and accountability hit the loss-of-trust crisis right at the core. Taking on the responsibility for consistency restores a sense of order, and a regular system of accountability helps to reassure that this fragile new order will remain—or that changes, when they occur, can be more readily foreseen.

Let us tie these concepts of consistency and accountability specifically with the use of the boundary limits and clear behavioral guidelines mentioned earlier. When loss of trust occurs, there has been a breach of the existing contract or understanding that brought the partners together. I use the word *contract* intentionally since this process is not much different from contracts of the legal kind. Loss of trust means that the couple's initial working agreement is now either invalid or so badly damaged that it cannot sustain the relationship. The goal of rewriting behavioral guidelines and establishing boundaries more clearly is to create a temporary, experimental agreement. The role of consistency and accountability to the guidelines is to ascertain whether trust can be rebuilt and the relationship restored. If both partners can adhere to this new limited agreement for their relationship, despite past unreliability and the current mistrust, this renewed cooperation can, presumably, serve as the groundwork for broadening the trust.

Consistency—the regular, repetitive performance of the behaviors set as guidelines—indicates the partners' willingness to follow through. It is also a clear observable measure of the extent of their caring about the relationship. Thus, it is crucial that the partners take great care that, regardless of circumstance or excuse, the agreed-upon behaviors are carried out. If the agreement was that the spouses will not flirt with others, neither social embarrassment nor special beauty will serve as an excuse for violating that agreement. Moreover, if both partners are serious about this new commitment, each will continue fulfilling his or her half of the agreement irrespective of what the other does. For example, if both spouses agree not to use a charge card and one partner violates this agreement, the other's commitment to it must remain firm. This is no contingency agreement but an honest commitment to uphold one's word. "Well, how fair is that?" people ask when I describe what I mean about consistency. The answer is that the object here is to rebuild trust, not to be "fair." What's more, this is precisely where the importance of accountability begins to come into this program.

Psychologist Sheldon Kopp[9] has written that he is sure that to be "inside someone else's head" is, by definition, to go crazy. Clearly, one person's view of reality can differ radically from the experience or interpretation of another. For this reason, consistency without a regular system of accountability is unworkable. In the absence of an ongoing, regular process of review one partner may be thinking that the behavior guidelines are being followed in a consistent fashion while the other may maintain that nothing at all has changed. Accountability allows both partners the opportunity to review in a structured fashion their own behaviors and those of their partner and to voice their feelings about each other's progress in following the agreement. This helps to modify the kind of random criticism that is often experienced as complaining, nitpicking, or whining.

Accountability, as I use the concept in marital therapy, calls for a daily or weekly meeting, the central purpose of which is to evaluate how the agreements reached or boundaries and behaviors outlined are being handled. It is a sort of checks-and-balances system that furthers trust. To the extent that partners take this time to review situations—especially where already agreed upon behaviors did not occur—they further create an atmosphere of trust. While you may not always recognize or understand your partner's behavior, if you know you can rely on your partner's willingness to account for and explain that behavior, a feeling of trust can be cemented. In addition, you will both need to know how the other thinks you are doing so that you can become aware of anything you may have unintentionally missed.

Besides either daily or weekly checkup times, accountability is enhanced by a monthly review, which differs from the checkup times in that it provides an opportunity for renegotiation. Once the initial agreement has been made, partners can benefit from asking for clarification and reviewing the behaviors that have actually occurred. However, renegotiating terms of the agreement before the passage of a month's time is destructive and confusing.

At the monthly review partners can vent complaints, fight some more, and, finally, negotiate for needed changes. This is the time to examine failures and to look at which behaviors need to be added—slowly—to the preceding arrangements. It is a time to consider whether enough trust has been built to continue or expand—or whether it is time to terminate the relationship.

THE "WHOLE MESSAGE": ADVANCES IN HONESTY

Another activity that can be useful in rebuilding trust is to engage in open, honest discussion throughout the reconciliation period. *Openness* and *honesty* are commonly used but misunderstood terms. My experience with group therapy has led me to believe that most people think being honest or open means "spilling their guts" in a sort of uncensored confession. Within the context of our discussion of trust and managing a marital crisis, I have something different in mind, specifically, a kind of openness and honesty that can help foster trust. I am referring to a way of sharing one's feelings and thoughts that helps explicit contracts and accountability reviews keep things out in the open. The goal of openness in this light is not necessarily to confess one's wrongdoings. Nor is it to tell someone everything you've always wanted to say to them but didn't. Instead, it is a particular style of communication that Walter Kempler[10] calls the "whole message." The whole message is simply that: a complete and authentic statement of one's feelings and thoughts. It is this combination of what one is prepared to say and what one usually does not say, out of embarrassment or shame, that is an especially helpful tool in rebuilding trust. When the whole message is given, there are no secrets left to create doubt. The "fullness" of a whole message is in making the speaker, at that moment, fully known to the listener.

For example, as I wrote those lines about the whole message, I was saying to the reader "I want you to understand the utility of this idea and respect me for presenting such a useful notion." But this is only half of the message. The other half is "I sure like explaining the utility of the whole message. It's a shame that Kempler discovered it before I did. I hope the reader credits me as much as him."

An example of a common whole message in marital therapy might be: "Yes, we agreed that I would call you at four o'clock each day. I didn't because it's another one of your unreasonable demands." In order to complete the message, one might add: "I also didn't call because having to make a formal agreement to be responsible makes me realize how irresponsible I have been. To have come to this point is terribly embarrassing."

In summary, then, to deal effectively with a marital crisis, there are two matters of concern: (1) appreciating the special features of a crisis and (2) assessing and rebuilding lost trust. To review, dealing with the key features of a crisis requires the following:

1. Distinguishing between that which can be controlled and that which cannot.
2. Avoiding placing or accepting personal blame.
3. Accepting that which you are helpless to change.
4. Allowing for venting hurt and anger.
5. Negotiating for changes with a sharper eye toward what really can be changed.
6. Using time-outs when rage gets the best of you.
7. Remembering to keep communication and changes made in crisis modest and simple.
8. Recalling that the goal of crisis is to survive the crisis intact in order to meet what life has to offer next.

The keys to rebuilding trust are the following:

1. Making implicit expectations explicit.
2. Deciding on limits and identifying which behaviors are below the belt.
3. Contracting for minimal and mutually understood new guidelines.
4. Writing out this contract and setting times for review and renegotiation.
5. Being accountable.
6. Being consistent—no matter what.
7. Using "whole messages" in communication.

We have seen that the disruption caused by a crisis requires specific measures to restore peace at home. In the next chapter we will discuss more general attitudes that can help maintain that peace.

Chapter 10

THE VALUE OF CONFLICT
AND BALANCE

Not until we are lost do we begin to understand ourselves.

—Henry David Thoreau

Often, couples come into therapy complaining that they argue regularly but that little is resolved. When I listen and watch chronically argumentative couples, I often find that they share at least two characteristics. One is that neither person seems to be clear as to the issue at hand. Each may shout, insult, and reiterate with fervor but without an understanding of what the fight is meant to resolve. The second characteristic common to such couples is their tendency to believe that agreement or a common consensus ought to be a given.

ACCEPTING CONFLICT: APPRECIATING THE PROCESS

I usually press a couple to define their issue and to fight it out openly and fairly on the assumption that doing so offers both partners a chance to learn more about what the other actually needs. Yet I commonly encounter a reluctance on their part to do so. I am typically told that they don't like to argue, even though they were having frequent unfocused arguments, predictable in both content and outcome, before seeking therapy. This reluctance seems rooted in the expectation that being in the same boat— being in love, being married, and having children—should neutralize any real differences. In short, couples expect togetherness, or harmony.

Actually, the pursuit of togetherness in marriage is a process, not a product. Harmony between husband and wife cannot be bought or guaranteed by gifts from parents. Nor can it be bought at the marital therapist's office. Even when it is achieved, a period of peacefulness will not remain so. Time and stress will inevitably chase it away, and it must be pursued again.

At the heart of an earned or pursued togetherness is an open-mindedness that is vitalizing, as opposed to a smug closedness that is deadly to relationships. Innocent curiosity breathes life into relationships whereas its absence freezes the couple in a deadly cold. Mutual curiosity creates a bond that can restore peace to many a troubled household. When couples find themselves at peace with each other, curiosity abounds: "I wonder how he looks in a suit"; "I wonder what she's like when she's angry?" As couples lose a sense of peace or ease, their curiosity diminishes. Now inner thoughts are more like "I just know what he will say!" or "I just know she will be angry!" A key to pursuing peace is to keep an open mind about the current trouble. Peace is so easily lost or becomes more inaccessible when partners stop asking questions and presume to know each other's intentions and feelings.

Maintaining open-mindedness is not easy. When people are disappointed, hurt, or angry, they typically close up and resort to a kind of reductionist thinking, which is almost the antithesis of open-mindedness. Doubts and suspicions congeal into certainties. Once reductionistic thinking takes hold, there is no gray, only black-and-white extremes—with black usually predominating. This thinking is reflected in comments like "You always . . ."; "You never . . ."; and "Our marriage will never . . . ." This lack of open-mindedness virtually guarantees that lost peace will stay lost for a longer period of time. In contrast, it is when the couple begins to question in earnest that peace begins its return; as the sages have noted: "A wise man's question is itself half the answer."

Conflict is more than a mere imbalance. Just as learning to deal with losing one's balance on a bicycle is essential to learning to maintain balance, so is learning to deal with conflict vital to maintaining togetherness. When conflict occurs, it is usually accompanied by feelings of disappointment and other negative feelings. This is because, as we have noted, people often tend to expect harmony and therefore find conflict annoying. Because of their annoyance, they approach conflict as an undesirable development and deal with it by attacking, blaming, or shaming their partner in conflict, by defending their own needs, or by withdrawing from the conflict. The first approaches—attacking, blaming, and shaming—all tend to put others on guard and often create new problems because of the animosity they add to the conflict. Defending merely accents an already polarized situation; defending one's own needs in the face of conflict, although a natural reaction, fails to allow either party to move toward something more peaceful. Finally, withdrawing is a form of denial; while it provides temporary relief from the conflict, it leaves matters unchanged, to be reencountered at a later time.

People who use these unsuccessful approaches toward conflict share a basic similarity of attitude in that they are not accepting of conflict, only reactive to it. They seem to be saying "Conflict is an awful inconvenience. The best I can hope for is to make it go away." What they lack is an acceptance of the inevitability of conflict between people who care for each other and of its necessity for the healthy development of the relationship. In most cases a couple's capacity to resolve conflicts productively is more essential to their well-being than is sexual compatibility.

In contrast to the view that conflict is a bad thing and reacting is all we can do stands the notion that conflict can be a catalyst for deepening relationships by actively engaging the partners. This is not to say that I believe couples should go around looking for a fight; what I mean is that when differing needs produce a conflict, that conflict must be acted upon and "worked through."

PROCESSING: THE POSITIVE FACE OF CONFLICT

"Working through" or "processing" is one of the most valuable tools ever used in psychotherapy. In the context of conflict between couples processing implies two basic ideas: (1) people's needs and feelings must be affirmed and accepted, even if only temporarily and (2) when needs or feelings are understood, placed in context, and seen as part of a process, they can be addressed in a more productive fashion. Working through conflict, then, effects a major shift from reacting to a conflict to acting on it. This shift occurs when both partners recognize that acting on conflict involves a serious attempt to understand and address their needs. As a result, the competitiveness and tension normally created by the "reacting mode" to conflict can ease.

Easing begins as soon as the reflexive urge to compete subsides. When couples can be assured that their needs will not be ignored or discounted, they are able to begin letting go of the urge to compete. In place of competition comes a readiness to gather important information and a curiosity about the needs at hand. This is one of the signs that a couple has begun to "engage the conflict" rather than react to it. For instance, it is important for partners to know what the other's needs actually are; they also need to know which needs are urgent. Further, it is helpful to understand to what extent certain needs feel especially pressing. Sometimes a person's self-esteem may be on the line in connection with a certain need whereas he or she may feel less intense about another need. For example, one woman felt emotionally crushed when her husband would continue phone conversations when she asked for his attention. This behavior made her feel that her efforts as his wife were taken for granted. She brought to the relationship some large personal issues about being ignored, but if her husband had forgotten her birthday, it would not have been nearly as painful as feeling ignored under the circumstances described.

By inquiring about each other's needs, couples begin the process of understanding and working through conflict and thus move closer to pursuing peace. They can learn which needs are emotional priorities. If couples can talk about their needs with the realization that needs require understanding, as opposed to justification, they can build trust and caring. When people feel that their needs are accepted without justification, they tend to feel valued and become more relaxed. In this relaxed atmosphere, where there is less fear that needs will be either ignored or dismissed, it becomes easier to decide when and how these needs can be met. Once partners are assured that they will each get serious attention, they become capable of examining whether what they need must be fulfilled immediately or whether it can be delayed. That is, an additional benefit of the emotional safety provided by the working-through process is that people are better able to distinguish between vital needs and mere desires or whims. In short, people in this process can get a clearer, truer, deeper sense of themselves and of each other.

The kind of emotional shift we have described, which can be created by the working-through process, is not unlike what sometimes happens during a run on a store or bank, when there is an anticipated shortage of supplies or money. If customers expect a store to deplete its supply of some staple, they try to buy up as much as they can carry; if depositors fear that a bank will fail, they rush to withdraw their assets. If the store owner or banker is able to reassure everyone that there will be enough to go around or that new supplies are expected soon, the situation becomes more relaxed. Once people feel that they are no longer threatened, they find it easier to resist hoarding and to negotiate. So it is with couples who enter the process of working through conflict. The process gives the vital assurance that the needs of both partners have a place; it enables a couple to look more carefully and thoughtfully at what they do need, and, finally, it changes the doubts a couple may have had about their suitability for each other so that the only serious questions are when and how their needs will be incorporated into the relationship.

CONFLICT: IMBALANCE AND EQUILIBRIUM

Conflict is a natural state of imbalance in that it occurs in families where someone's needs or feelings are receiving too little or too much attention. Once the imbalance is accepted instead of feared, the couple can begin to right itself. Awareness of how needs or feelings are out of kilter can lead to a solution that is more stable. Understanding the causes of imbalance is, then, essential to restoring a happier balance.

Togetherness in a relationship also requires an aesthetic appreciation and respect for differences. In our automated and hectic lifestyles, convenience often demands uniformity. This attitude frustrates the pursuit of harmony. Intimacy thrives on a blending or mixing of differences. Vital relationships are rarely black and white, where, for example, one person always leads and the other always follows. Instead, in solid marriages the partners appreciate the value of gray. They trust that neither has to "win" in order for a solution to conflict to be satisfying. Reaching compromise, where both individuals feel attended to, is neither simple nor convenient. What is required is patient listening, trust, and a willingness to have each one's needs reflected in the solution. There are no instant compromises. Compromises require awareness of each other and the capacity to take some joy in the sharing—the very essence of being a responsible partner. The ability to enjoy shades of gray and a commitment to work at finding them adds freshness and mutual pride that the sameness of black-and-white solutions do not afford. A happy marriage, then, is like a cloth woven of many shades and colors, reflecting the specialness, harmony, and mutual respect of the partners.

Formulas for marital harmony and togetherness need to contain a balance and blend of need-satisfying actions. Yet the solution goes beyond reluctant compromise; it goes beyond recognizing and honoring the rights of both partners. In addition, the intimacy and marital harmony of the union of husband and wife contains a spiritual synergy. Resolving imbalances alone only stops marital arguments or fights, but finding a peace that reflects a satisfaction of the emotional needs of both husband and wife allows each to reach new emotional heights. Together they can reach a level of happiness and energy beyond what either could have achieved alone.

The next chapter will take up the theme of togetherness and mutual satisfaction on the physical plane.

Chapter 11

SEXUALITY

And Adam knew Eve his wife.

Genesis 4:1

THE SEX–CLOSENESS CONUNDRUM

Modern man seems to have developed a particular attraction to anything instant or automatic. It is in the area of sexuality that this penchant has been taken to especially damaging extremes. Couples have come to expect instant intimacy. Husband and wife may exist in two entirely different worlds, but upon entering the bedroom they expect to establish instant sexual compatibility. What's more, if their sexual expertise is not automatically excellent, both fear that something is seriously wrong with their relationship. Couples may be emotionally very distant and feel but little concern about it; yet when their sexual experience is below par, a sense of alarm sets in. Actually, it is when couples begin to show as much alarm for the degree of emotional distance in the relationship outside

153

the bedroom as for the degree of sexual dysfunction that sexual intimacy begins to improve.

The importance of emotional distance in sexual relationships was especially clear in the case of a woman I treated some years ago. She was part of the large single adult component of our society. We spent some months reviewing her relationships with men. After working through a particularly painful failed relationship, she turned to me and said half jokingly, "I think I am going to give up sexual relations for meaningful human contact." In ten years of active sexual relations, the one element clearly missing from this woman's life was meaningful human contact, that is, consistent emotional closeness.

What is it, then, that allows for meaningful human contact to occur? How is consistent emotional closeness established? Much can be gleaned from studying the concept behind the word *to know*, as in the biblical phrase "and Adam knew Eve his wife." For example, the Hebrew term *layda* (to know) implies more than the euphemistic "knowing in the biblical sense." Rather, *layda* implies an active ongoing and mutual kind of understanding.

KNOWING YOUR PARTNER

The well-known Talmudic scholar Rabbi Joseph B. Soloveichik[11] says that one must actively pursue knowing in order to reach causative personal awareness. Applying this understanding of the word *to know* to Adam and Eve, what emerges is that intimacy defines sexual behavior. Mutual knowing, or intimacy, provides the basis upon which physical relationships are best built, a truth recognized by a wise patient, who once said to her husband, "You have to learn to share my feelings before you will share my bed again."

Meaningful human contact may now best be described as a togetherness forged by *layda*. When couples maintain an active understanding of each other's feelings, needs, and struggles, they create an environment where meaningful human contact can occur.

This type of intimacy, which begins outside the bedroom, carries an emotional closeness that enhances physical closeness. Sexual functioning is usually healthiest in a climate of consistent mutual awareness.

THE BEDROOM AS A MIRROR

In years of listening to a wide array of sexual problems, one maxim has emerged clearly for me: What happens inside the bedroom is usually a reflection of what is happening outside the bedroom. If there is distance, greed, a struggle for power, anger, or mistrust outside the bedroom, it will be replayed inside the bedroom, too. Such common sexual dysfunctions as premature ejaculation, vaginismus, secondary impotence, and loss of sexual interest are often traceable to some of these emotional difficulties.

Likewise, when couples who are physically in good health experience sexual problems, the place to begin healing is outside the bedroom. In order for one's sexual experience to improve, an improvement or adjustment in the relationship must often occur first. Actually, a large number of sexual dysfunctions are resolved when underlying, unexpressed angers or fears are discussed openly.

One of the most useful tools that I have found in the early phases of sexual dysfunction therapy centers on exploring just such feelings. I regularly suggest that the couple abstain from sex for a week and that they instead set aside a time and private place to meet each night. During this five- to ten-minute period, they are not to be interrupted by phones, children, or other distractions. During this period they are each required to put together two sentences: the first is to begin with the words "I did appreciate," the second with "I did not appreciate." This simple task and the discussions it can elicit will often allow for as yet unspoken feelings to become more accessible.

Suggested here are some additional steps that can be taken at home to improve a deteriorating sexual relationship. A first major step often requires a change in attitude. Men, in particular, commonly have an attitude toward sex that frequently results in conflict and difficulty. They seem to feel—and, at times, hold the stubborn conviction—that if sex becomes more frequent or better, relationship problems will disappear. This is, in fact, true for some men; if they can have their women accede to their sexual demands, they somehow feel more secure, flexible, and better able to respond to matters they would otherwise dismiss or avoid. For them, a change in sex, or sexual adjustment, apparently feels like a fundamental change in the relationship.

However, most couples experience this process in a reverse fashion, that is, sexual relations get better as relationship issues are resolved. The key point here is that a sexual issue is a two-person issue. It requires that the partners together deal with both symptoms and causes. "It's *your* problem" is a mistaken attitude, for even if it is just one partner's problem, both are going to have to deal with it together at some point if they want to stay together. Ultimately, a mutual adjustment is going to be necessary. Dealing together with a problem that involves togetherness just seems to make practical sense.

FIVE ATTITUDES THAT DESTROY INTIMACY

There are certain attitudes that kill sexual intimacy that deserve special mention at this point. The following are the most common destroyers of a good sexual relationship that I see in my office:

1. Confusing sex with emotional closeness
2. Confusing intercourse with making love
3. Confusing sexual imperfection with personal deficiency
4. Confusing the sexuality of the bedroom with the politics of the dinner table
5. Confusing sex with nature

That sex is the way to get close seems to be one of the most common messages around us today. If you cannot get close and feel close through sex, the implication is that you are a failure.

Actually, like all other propaganda, this message has some validity: having the capacity to feel a closeness during sex is a considerable benefit and a sign of emotional maturity. However, this attitude breeds an expectation that a normal couple should be able to find an almost immediate intimacy with sexual contact.

I have spent hours counseling "sexually liberated" men and women who insist that they will not go to bed with just anyone but who admit that they find their sexual encounters unfulfilling. Notwithstanding disclaimers to the contrary, many of these people seem to be trapped in the present-day myth of instant intimacy. It is almost as if they believed that the way to really get to know someone is to have a simultaneous orgasm or share a sexual fantasy. One personal satisfaction for me has been talking with teenagers who seem to understand better than some adults that sex can be just sex.

Deluged as we are by mass media-generated pop psychology and myths about sex, the special and distinct parts of our personalities are ignored or dismissed. Getting to know someone well enough to feel emotional closeness is a more difficult task than our pop culture would have us believe. Learning to accept another's shortcomings as well as strengths is harder than buying the myth of instant intimacy, which sex is popularly believed to offer.

This confusion between sex and closeness can create problems or frustration for couples. There is an expectation that if one partner offers sex, the other should feel or understand that a message of intimacy is being communicated. However, sexual gratification by itself is rarely a clear communication of closeness. I often see much pain in the eyes of patients whose predominant way of giving or receiving closeness has been through sexual expression. Often, this pain is manifested by an unspoken fear or open resentment. Insecurity, fear, and doubt in the face of the "closeness" achieved only through sex can result in a feeling of being used, a feeling expressed in the perennial question "Is my body all he or she wanted?"

Closeness involves a capacity for a mutually satisfying exchange. We feel close to others who both give and are able to receive what we offer. Sharing sexual pleasures is certainly a way to build close-ness. There is much to the unspoken word and the simple touch—but there is also a lot left out! And the void left, as we noted, is often filled with unsureness and doubt.

I don't intend to minimize the profound feelings that couples can experience in a nonverbal, sexual manner, but I do want to emphasize the need for couples to also express closeness and good feelings verbally. By speaking—whether simply or eloquently—to your partner about the closeness can enhance your relationship. It can help you avoid the pitfall of defining closeness solely in terms of sex. Likewise, touches, caresses, and hugs that don't carry a sexual message or demand are often useful. The benefits of an increased frequency of "nonsexual hugs" can be surprising. While a reassuring touch and a statement like "It feels good to be close" may not be as dramatic, they can often provide a more profound sense of closeness than mutual orgasm.

As their sexual awareness has increased, many patients report that, somehow, the benefits of "lovemaking" have decreased for them. I believe this is so because to them intercourse and love-making are seen as being synonymous. The exasperation I see on their faces assures me that the distinction between the two is easy to lose.

George, a bright thirty-three-year-old engineer, cried with a feeling of frustration when he confessed, "I tried everything I knew and just couldn't get her to respond." When I asked him about this frustrating experience in greater detail, it became clear that he was a sexual "technician." He was well-read, successful, and, in his own way, sensitive. Yet he approached the bedroom as if he were taking a final examination in automobile mechanics. Like so many others, his unsureness about closeness and his need for ac-ceptance resulted in his straining to do a "good job." His sensitivity toward people and his considerable capacity for caring gave way to an overbearing need to control. But George was no tyrant; he tried to control simply because he didn't want anything to go wrong.

By the time George made sure he had done a good job, his sexual partner felt dehumanized. He had treated her to carefully applied creams, a massage, and sensuous, accurately placed strokes. George had performed with the skill and devotion of a surgeon, but his partner felt like a packaged piece of meat. Both men and women, apologetic or fearful of being seen as sexually naive, can have an almost ritualized sexual experience, which leaves out the substance of their person. Had George verbalized his concerns, fears, and willingness to care about his partner, she would surely have felt more loved.

Making love requires a sharing of love. Sex that allows for this expression of love brings warmth and closeness. Without it, couples experience the loneliness and sterile futility that so well character-izes too much of today's culture. Making love can be an oasis in the barrenness of modern life while sex devoid of lovemaking is a violation of this remaining sanctuary of human intimacy.

SHAMING, BLAMING, AND SEXUAL FAILURE

Perhaps few things have consequences as far-reaching and devastating to the sexual life of a couple as blaming and shaming in the face of sexual failure. Couples in the early phases of their sexual relationship are especially prone to shaming, blaming, or accusing each other when their sexual experience has been unsat-isfactory. These attacks and statements of a partner's personal de-ficiency can be especially damaging.

Terms like *frigid* or *impotent* are best left to the doctors. Once one partner shifts into the role of lay diagnostician, a couple's equal partnership is terminated. It shifts from a relationship of equals to one of competitors and mutual exploiters. Once this shift occurs, it is difficult to reverse. More often than not, once blaming or name-calling begins, a cycle geared toward producing and main-taining emotional distance takes hold.

For some, the only way to deal with pain, disappointment, or hurt is to lash out in anger, as in blaming, sarcasm, or outright hostility. Such attacks can become a substitute for dealing with the pain that occurs when people who care for each other fail to meet personal expectations. As noted earlier, in dealing with hurt feelings the issues and needed changes must be kept separate from the rage of disappointment.

What is important to remember is that when your partner resorts to blaming, his or her disappointment is not necessarily directed at you. He or she may be having a problem that is causing the pain, disappointment, or hurt, a problem that is beyond conscious awareness or immediate control. To make personal attacks is to violate the trust that first brought you together. The key is to be clear about whether you want to work on change or destroy what is not as perfect as you might like or even deserve.

In the 1960s, a popular message on antiwar posters was "Make love, not war." Some couples I have seen in my office seem to have adopted an attitude expressed by a rewriting of this phrase, namely, "Make war *while* you are making love." For these couples the bedroom shifts from being a place for closeness and sharing and becomes, instead, a battlefield on which malicious struggles for control are waged. These battles sometimes come under the rubric of "sexual relations."

This common destroyer of sexual relationships occurs when power struggles are not resolved outside the bedroom. Such struggles can distort and ruin the most vibrant sexual relationship. In many ways the emotions of sex and aggression are separated by a rather fine line. Bringing family struggles for dominance into the bedroom tends to obscure the line between sex and aggression; once the distinction between the two is lost, the safety and tranquility of sexual intimacy can be lost as well.

Perhaps one of the most common examples of how couples fuse sex with aggression is when one partner suggests sex as a way to resolve a fight or to make up. Whatever issues, needs for change, hurts, and pains that surfaced during an argument are, in the thinking of such couples, supposed to evaporate with the sigh of orgasm. In fact, under such circumstances sex cannot help but be merged with the frustration and aggression left by unresolved problems and feelings.

On my wedding day my parents offered me the following words of wisdom: "Never go to bed angry." To this one might add, "Don't count on having a satisfying sexual experience when you are angry." What usually results is not peace. While there may be some physical release of tension, those issues that generated the tension are left to fester and breed resentments. Moreover, the potential haven of sexual intimacy is violated, a high price to pay for abandoning the patience and efforts needed to negotiate a resolution.

Finally, an even more pervasive destructive influence on a relationship is the assumption that sexual relations are automatically natural. I have seen couples whose relationship with each other is chaotic and filled with years of misunderstanding, disappointment, and resentment. They come into my office and fitfully exchange charges and countercharges. Invariably, as they conclude another fruitless emotional bloodbath, one will turn to the other and insist that sex is the key problem. What's more, one partner will sometimes add, "Sex is natural. Any dumb raccoon in the woods can do it; why can't we?"

Certainly, sexual relations between partners is natural. Sexual attraction and interest and the desire for sexual intimacy are natural human feelings. These facts, however, have little to do with sustaining a sexual relationship. As soon as a couple becomes involved in any relationship, sexual or otherwise, the entire array of needs and feelings enters the picture as well. Needs and feelings, along with the expectations they bring, are complex. To assume or expect that these differences will somehow naturally dissolve during a sexual relationship is at best seriously naive. It is important not to brand oneself as "unnatural" or "abnormal" if sustaining a sexual relationship is at times difficult.

People come together because they expect some mutual needs to be met. Needs, feelings, and expectations are vital parts of a sexual relationship. This fact makes sexual relationships simple, natural and a complexity in need of conscious mutual effort. In some way, all of us find our vulnerabilities in the sexual aspects of a relationship difficult. Keeping this idea in mind might help to treat yourself and your partner with some patience and gentleness, which is in itself half the battle.

As with other issues that disrupt peace in the home, sexual problems must not be ignored. You may try to run from such problems, but there is really no place to hide. Responsible struggle with the help of physicians or specially trained therapists can do much to limit both pain and damage to the relationship. Often, overcoming embarrassment and asking for help are the most important steps to be taken.

Chapter 12

THE MASKS OF FEAR

You can run, but you can't hide.

—Joe Louis

We are all scared, and spend most of our lives both hiding the fear and fighting it. In some cases fear freezes or paralyzes life energies for a period of time; in other cases it consumes an entire lifetime. Avoiding fear, simply not facing it, can detour one's direction in life. People may take detours to keep them safe from fear, only to find the specter of fear blocking their path.

A TALE OF FEAR, SHAME, AND PRIDE

Writer Ursula LeGuin[12] portrays a character named Ged whose story illustrates the compelling aspects of a life driven by fear and its psychological twin, shame. When we first meet Ged, he is a child known as Duny living in a lonely village on the island of Gont,

165

somewhere in "the storm-racked Northeast Sea, a land famous for wizards." Duny's mother has died in childbirth, and we learn that Duny was minimally fathered by a bronzesmith who was a "grim unspeaking man." Like so many children, Duny was left unprotected and unguided and, as such, vulnerable to fear. Although "there was no one to bring the child up in tenderness," Duny grew to be "tall and quick, loud and proud, and full of temper."

A critical person in this motherless child's life was his aunt. She was a sometimes foolish ignorant woman, who had a gift of magery. Mixed in with her knowledge of tricks, curses, and low magic was a beginner's understanding of how to call to and summon different animals by their "true names." The lonely Duny gravitated to his strange and interesting aunt, who saw a power in him that she began to develop by teaching him some of what she knew. What she did not know was that Duny was sneaking into her room and reading ancient spells from the books on her shelves, which drew more and more of his keen attention.

The transformation of Duny the waif into Ged the young wizard occurred under most unlikely circumstances. The entire island of Gont, including Ged's village, was attacked by a particularly brutal and fierce group of warriors; islands with better defenses had already fallen prey to these marauders. When they fell upon Ged's tiny village, the few defenders seemed to face certain death and the village awaited seemingly inevitable destruction. But that was when Duny decided to try one of the spells he had independently and secretly deciphered from his aunt's ancient texts. By calling to the fog in its "real name" Ged managed to ensnarl the invaders in a thick mist that caused them to be driven off the jagged cliffs of Gont into the sea. Then, exhausted by the unforeseen strain of employing such a powerful spell (a fact of magery unknown to his aunt), Ged fell into a coma-like state. Even as knowledge of the young wizard's heroics was spreading across the islands, a master wizard was summoned to heal him, since his aunt had correctly concluded that he had "overspent his power."

It was this master wizard, Ogion, who both set the spent young wizard on his feet and revealed his true name to be Ged. True names were very important in the world inhabited by Ged, because it was only by knowing the true name of someone or something that that entity's powers could be understood. Ogion not only understood Ged's true name but also took keen notice of the 13-year-old wizard's potential. He easily convinced Ged's father to allow the boy to come and live with him so that he could develop the gift for wizardry that he had displayed.

Ged's stay with Ogion was to be short-lived. He was filled with the unspoken hope that Ogion, with his spells and magic, would free him from the emotional shackles of being an unwanted, afraid, motherless child. Instead, Ogion turned out to be a steady, calm, and seemingly ordinary goatherd whose principal teaching was that "mastery is nine times patience." Driven by his own impatience, Ged found himself boasting to a young girl from a nearby town who teased him about the powers that such a famous young wizard ought to have. Her challenge that he perform some spell or charm led Ged to a hidden shelf of Ogion's library. This time, however, Ged's independent research was interrupted by his mentor: Ogion warned his fear- and shame-driven disciple, "Before you speak or do, you must know the price that is to pay!" Driven by his shame, Ged cried, "How am I to know these things when you teach me nothing?" Sensing that Ged was too insecure to learn from silent thoughtful observation, Ogion arranged for his pupil's acceptance at the school for wizards on the Isle of Roke—the Harvard of wizard schools. There the precocious and driven Ged excelled; within a year's time he was studying on the level of students who had been enrolled for several years. It was on Roke that Ged changed the course of his young life irrevocably. In response to unending harsh teasing by one older student Ged unleashed a spell to summon a spirit from the dead, but he was so undone by the challenge to prove himself equal, if not superior, that he ignored the lessons about balance that he had been taught.

The terrible spell uttered by Ged caused a serious upheaval in the spiritual worlds. He was suddenly overtaken by a dark shadow so powerful that the Archmage of Roke himself had to fight a deadly battle to subdue this terrific force, a battle in which the

Archmage was killed. It took nearly a year for Ged to recover from this encounter with the shadow, after which he, a highly skilled—but shaken—wizard, left Roke.

Ged's travels took him across the then-known world; he wandered restlessly, using his talents and power to slay menacing dragons and monsters. As Ged's fame as a hero followed him around the globe, so too did the spirit and presence of the shadow that was unleashed at Roke. No matter the number of slain dragons, saved towns, or successful acts of wizardry skill, Ged could not escape the menacing, eerie pursuit of the shadow. Sadly, Ged's reputation and good name as a heroic mage were diminished by his shameful dread and retreat from his own shadow.

In the end Ged finally encountered his shadow of fear and shame, but not until he had wasted much of his life and energy in avoidance. He was not able to enjoy his own talents, relax with the many interesting people he met, or bask in their appreciation of his efforts and personal charm until he could free himself from the shadow. Ordinary men and women, too, can be driven to excel, achieve, and take great risks, all the while propelled by unresolved personal fear and shame.

The truly scary thing about fear is that while it both shapes and distorts us in profound ways, the fear itself is usually invisible. Fear is an oft-unspoken enemy that is, nevertheless, also the raison d'être for many partnerships. Even as small children, we form bonds with other children to explore unfamiliar places, encounter new experiences, and endure scary movies or amusement rides. Fear forces us to reach out with a suddenness and intensity that sets it apart from other emotions.

As we have noted, fear and bonding go together. The reassuring hand of a friend, parent, or older brother or sister extended at a time of fright is a gesture some never forget. Yet in marriage, people often repeat the old horror movie scenario in which the place of refuge becomes more horrific than the impending danger from without. It is this hidden aspect of fear that causes such trouble for individuals and the relationships they form.

THE FALSE SELF: A MASK OF FEAR

Masks are a cultural symbol of fear. They personify both the strangeness that is fear's seen face and the secrecy that gives fear such power. Contemporary advances in psychoanalysis and the psychotherapy of the so-called borderline condition have added considerable understanding to what is known about fear. In particular, writers such as D. W. Winnicott[13] and Alice Miller[14] have shown how fear of shame or abandonment can cause people to develop a "false self," a kind of personality mask, in order to protect themselves. These masks help people put on a face they hope will keep peace with others while also affording protection from the danger itself. Sadly, many beautiful, expressive, lively faces, that is, personalities, remain trapped behind the very masks that were once donned as protection.

Many of these masks become more understandable to us as we get older and wiser. We recognize that the once fearsome mask of the bully hides a shameful cowardice and that the hard face of callousness is sometimes only a disguise for those who fear exposure of their tender vulnerabilities. Other masks escape detection until stress, time, or life's travails expose a truer self, one that oozes through the cracks of falsehood like the hideous mummies that emerge from their dusty crypts in an old monster movie.

When Sun met Gary, she thought she would be safe forever. He was a wisecracking, highly competent officer who stood out even in the company of his own outlandish buddies. It was not his stature that set Gary apart but, rather, the calm, almost cold gaze that seemed to never leave his face. In Sun's world of the turmoil and unpredictability of war, Gary's eyes were a blue oasis. Even his outspoken cynicism, which made Gary sound as if he did not trust anyone, seemed to reinforce Sun's sense that safety followed this man like a shadow.

At first Sun greeted Gary's attentions toward her with all the caution that a woman in wartime could muster. She refused his repeated invitations to go dancing, because she never took them seriously. His boldly open racial slurs made it clear that he held little regard for anyone but his own kind. It was Gary's curious persistence that ultimately weakened Sun's resolve: he never got angry in the face of the most terse of Sun's refusals and appeared even more good-natured with each new invitation. Finally, Sun dropped her guard and let herself feel the protection and love of this seemingly hardened man. When Gary left Vietnam, he continued his oft-repeated, tender, teasing "threat" to never see Sun again. Sun was astonished but ready when the ever-resourceful Gary arranged for her tickets and papers to join him in the United States.

Fairy tale turned to nightmare very shortly. Gary could not hold a job. He squandered his assets on ill-conceived real estate deals, on a poorly managed limousine service, and on schooling he never completed. In the beginning Sun attributed Gary's failures to bad luck. When he began to abuse her, she feared she had indeed married a demon. Gary's former brazen and arrogant manner had given way to paranoia, unpredictable mood swings, and brutality.

Like many other victims of war-induced personality deterioration, Gary's pre-wartime weaknesses had burst through in the face of peacetime adjustments. Without the background drama of a life-or-death setting, Gary's fears of his own inadequacies and uncertainties were in danger of being exposed. This perceived danger, which Gary thought he had overcome in the army, now returned, leaving him with nowhere to hide. In Gary's mind losing the air of invulnerability was a terrible unmasking. Without his mask of imperturbability Gary feared being seen as less than ordinary. To him this carried the threat of being unnoticed and ultimately left friendless and alone. The more frightened and impulsive Gary became, the poorer the judgments and decisions he made. Bad judgments begot failure. Gary's ultimate fear of failure inflamed his mistrust of Sun and ignited bouts of physical and emotional abuse. A stranger in a new land, Sun was a total loss. Worse, she felt paralyzed by the self-doubt she suffered as a result of Gary's horrific transformation. This unmasking turned her oasis into a violently unsettling mirage.

The human spirit can learn to deal with life's disappointments. That spirit, however, is sometimes broken or crippled when the disappointment seems to emerge without warning and comes in the form of shattered trust. When Gary reluctantly entered treatment, Sun was unable to rejoin the relationship. She eventually forgave Gary's abuse but was unable to recover from the terrible unmasking of her erstwhile protector. Gary was now left alone to face his demons without an appreciative audience to distract him.

One with a cynical view of human nature would insist that in love, as in business, the buyer must beware: nothing is as it appears and people are not what they seem to be. Yet even allowing for the kind of cynicism that may serve to balance the Pollyannaish optimism of romance, there is something about seeing a loved one in a black light that shakes one's very grip on reality. Carl Jung was a talented observer of both overt and covert human nature. He understood the darker side, the more hidden side of personality, which he called the "shadow." There is comfort to be taken in Jung's concept of the shadow: we all have one and we can live fuller, richer lives only by becoming better acquainted with our own shadow.

YOUR SHADOW: KNOW IT OR TRIP OVER IT!

The heroine in playwright David Mamet's[15] *House of Games* is an example of someone whose alienation from her darker self causes her downfall. Margaret Ford is a psychiatrist with a hidden bent for risk and the challenge of danger. She becomes intrigued, almost to the point of enchantment, by a devil-may-care con man. His life is lived on the edge while her own is wearing and predictable. In the end, Margaret is ensnared by the allure of danger and becomes involved in a robbery and murder. These events affect her life, both situationally and emotionally, to the point where she is transformed. When people seek to mask or ignore needs or feelings that seem not to fit their desired image, they are vulnerable to having those same unheeded voices one day take the wheel instead of the back seat and direct their life.

Intimacy, both physical and emotional, is but one facet of marriage that has the potential strength to crack even the most well-worn mask. Consider the mask worn by Sue: after both of Sue's parents died, before she reached puberty, she lived with her two older brothers and a rather ineffectual aunt and became "one of the boys." She had a way of setting men so much at ease with her friendly smile that she was usually treated as a longtime friend. One such buddy was Tom, and when Sue became engaged to him, the entire neighborhood felt itself to be part of the celebrating family. Every guy who knew Sue wished he could be in Tom's place: the lucky stiff would be spending his life with the most outgoing, uninhibited girl around.

Clearly, Tom felt that his life would be free of the "girl mood-iness" that plagued his friends. Sue not only enjoyed watching softball but could also hit as well as any man her size. Tom was sure that marriage to Sue would be like living with a best buddy—who happened to be beautiful and desirable. Sue's unmasking came when Tom took to staring into her eyes; she couldn't get him to stop those searching, piercing gazes that had annoyingly become part of the ritual of their lovemaking. So unnerved was Sue by Tom's staring that she would lock him out of the bedroom, letting him in only if he promised "to get right to it and to stop playing mind games."

For his part, Tom was baffled. After the hoopla of the wedding, he began to appreciate Sue even more than before. To him she was a miraculous thing of beauty; he wondered how anyone could be as terrific as Sue. The staring was, at first, completely unintentional. One night, as they lay together, Tom could see Sue's pupils dilate; although he couldn't tell what her eyes said, Tom was some-how transfixed by what he saw. The staring that so annoyed and infuriated Sue was a real searching that felt compelling to Tom. Finally, Sue confessed, amid the first tears that Tom had ever seen her shed, that she was scared to death; all her life everyone had so readily bought her easy smile and seemingly effortless friendliness

that Sue was able to avoid developing close relationships and confronting her needs for nurturance, solace, and intimacy. Somehow,
Tom had gotten curious, which left Sue in a state of anxiety that
she called "white fright." The couple entered therapy, and the
long-hidden sadness of this long ago-orphaned little girl would
erupt into uncontrollable sobs each time an opportunity for intimacy presented itself.

THE FACES OF FEAR

For couples to deal effectively with fear and its manifold masks,
it is useful to have not only a basic understanding of how fear works
but also a healthy respect for its complexities. Let us begin by
noting that there are different kinds of fear. In the cases just described, fear served to mask Gary's self-perceived inadequacies and
Sue's long-hidden inner sadness and self-alienation. Reference was
made earlier to Jung's concept of the shadow, in which unwanted
parts of the self are believed to take on a personality all their own.
At their core, both our examples show the person's concerns about
personal acceptability, abandonment, and failure and show how
emotions, choices, and responsibilities were avoided. Intellectually,
we can understand these clues about fear, even as they evade our
grasp in our own everyday emotional experience.

Panic or Phobic Fear

One kind of fear that bears special mention is one that presents
itself in the form of panic or terror. What sets this type of fear
apart from the others is that it is so compelling, overwhelming, and
confusing. When people experience a "phobic anxiety" attack, or
what we will call a panic attack, they invariably feel as if they are
either going mad or are about to die. As extreme as this description
may sound, it fails to convey the shock that a panic attack presents
to the sufferer. In addition, so very little is known or written about

such attacks that the person who has one is likely to feel very much alone and entirely strange.

When one partner suffers from a panic disorder it will likely affect the other. Like the other forms of fear that we have mentioned, panic attacks are usually hidden, most often behind a veil of excuses that are used to protect the phobic person from either potentially fearful situations or to create an alibi to explain a current or past attack. I have seen couples in my practice who have terrible arguments about never going out socially or about avoiding vacation plans until husband or wife finally confesses this disabling condition to the other. Typically, people who suffer from a panic disorder feel that no one could understand what they themselves are quite ashamed to describe or are simply so overwhelmed and terrified by the attacks that they literally cannot find words to express what has happened to them.

Panic attacks also produce changes in both thought and behavior. Not unlike those in physical crises—patients with a severe illness, soldiers in wartime, hostages, or survivors of a physical disaster—those who experience panic attacks are likely to adopt a mind-set that accompanies a crisis, which includes three main features: (1) shortsightedness, (2) impulsivity, and (3) wandering or circular thinking, which lacks a consistent focus. When in real or perceived danger, people tend to narrow their perspective and to concern themselves only with the immediate future. For someone suffering from panic attacks this may mean that the only decisions that can be made are the most immediate; thus, it may be difficult to plan vacations, finances, or even an evening out, since the panic-prone person is more focused on how he or she is going to make it through the aftermath of the most recent attack or on how to avoid the one that lies ahead.

The Silent Pain of a Panic Disorder

Impulsive thoughts and tendencies can also imprison those who suffer from a panic disorder. All kinds of irrational ideas, which are often most extreme, may pop into their mind. These impulsive ideas may relate to such events as suicide, divorce, or leaving town, even though there may be no rational reason for these to be of concern. In fact, it is their reacting to or attempting to process these sudden thoughts that often leaves panicked persons so immobile. Such impulsive thoughts absorb both time and energy; because of their extreme nature, they tend to cause a fixedness of attention and can be as mesmerizing as a traffic accident is to gapers. What one considers while caught in this thinking state is often so shockingly extreme that the mind itself seems to become almost frozen in amazement.

When obsessing sets in, the nature of panic-related thinking can change from fixity to flux. Obsessing is fear-driven thinking; it causes one's mind to meander in a spiral-like cycle of "what ifs." Having experienced the emotional disaster of a panic attack, a person tends to wonder what will come next. "What if I never come out of the panic?" is a common question from phobic anxiety sufferers. Propelled by adrenalin, the worrying about the possibilities of the dreaded "what ifs" seems unending. Each "what if" challenges the mind to create a solution for the next impending catastrophe. Locked in this mental maze, the person treats every possible "what if" as a certain eventuality: all possible dangers demand solutions, without which there is neither respite nor safety. And each possible solution must be perfect and airtight so that nothing else can go wrong. This level of perfectionistic expectation only gives rise to an acute awareness of the most subtle of flaws, which then becomes the focus of the next threatening problem. As each answer becomes the next problem, a spiral of increasing panic and a sense of being trapped sets in. Small wonder that people who suffer from panic appear to be stuck; they are unable to fight their way out of this proverbial paper bag of fear. What's more, I have come to understand, people in the throes of this cycle believe themselves to be engaged in problem solving when they are actually frantically sawing sawdust.

From the standpoint of observable behavior, panic may appear as laziness, lack of interest, complaining, or compulsive activity. Laziness or lack of interest are often coupled with a negativity that can put an automatic kibosh on almost any kind of planned family activity. Complaining can be a way to avoid doing anything new— and therefore unanticipated and potentially dangerous; claims of inconvenience or expense or complaints of aches and pains are common defenses against the potential threat of change. Flurries of compulsive activity sometimes punctuate the doldrums of risk avoidance. These "activities" range from the compulsive use of alcohol to overeating or shopping binges. While these spurts would seem to be a break from the passivity of obsessive periods, compulsive behaviors do not provide relief. Instead, this kind of "fear doing" tends to leave a feeling of emptiness because little, if any, directed or meaningful activity has been accomplished. This can be particularly discouraging since compulsive actions usually consume great amounts of energy, money, and time. Often, the disappointment and depletion that compulsive episodes leave in their wake become the breeding ground for the next generation of panic thoughts.

Taming Panic

Some twenty percent of the adult population in the United States struggles with some form of panic disorder for reasons that remain a mystery of the body and the mind. If your partner suffers from a panic disorder, or parts of the cycle just described, you can be helpful in any one of three ways. First, simply pointing out to your partner that your life together is being affected can be a real help. Typically, people who suffer panic distress deny the problem out of great shame and worry. Being approached by their partner in a way that says "We must and we will get through this" is a major positive step for them. Second, avoid blaming or shaming your partner for having the problem, but find some way to be firm in insisting, without adding more pain, that your partner get relief. Finally, let your partner know that there is specific help available. Claire Weeks,[16] a noted expert on phobic conditions and panic disorders, has written an immensely helpful, easy-to-understand book entitled *Peace from Nervous Suffering*. I routinely insist that my patients with panic disorders read this book—over and over

again. In her book Dr. Weeks identifies four central principles that
realistically and pragmatically allow people to live with this disorder
in a safe and sane way:

1. Face the fear; don't run from it.
2. Accept the panic attacks; don't fight them.
3. "Float" through the attacks; don't listen to your mind during an attack.
4. Let time pass; the attacks always go away, in time.

These principles run against the natural instinct we have to
fight fear or panic. Actually, it is in denying, bargaining with, and
fighting panic that the cycle is fed. The greater the resistance one
offers, the more the body reacts by producing adrenalin. As a result
of the tension created by resistance, the sense of danger and the
experience of panic become more intense. Paradoxically, the more
one is able to surrender to the panic, like a judo expert leaning
into a fall, the less the damage incurred. For those who are unable
to work these steps, a psychiatric consultation focused on evaluating
the need for medication for the panic disorder presents another
viable option. Struggling with panic, without help and proper information, is like being caught in a giant roll of flypaper. Healing
help, as we have noted, is both available and vital; it is important
that the couple not become exhausted in desperate frustration.

In examining the varied masks of fear, we have seen how damaging unseen fears can be. Fears of abandonment, social rejection,
failure and, in the case of panic, even a fear of fear itself can all
distort one's life. Sometimes this distortion takes the form of hiding
or of an unrelenting drive for success or achievement. Fear may
be accompanied by shame, or it may be accelerated by the body's
own chemistry. Whether it motivates obviously compulsive behaviors or visible sweating and shakes or hides in private and unseen
terrors, fear presents a central threat to couples.

FEAR AND INTIMACY

The greatest threat fear poses to couples is its capacity to destroy intimacy. One who is caught up in self-doubts and concerns

is able to relate to another in only a superficial way. Even though personal ghosts usually remain hidden in relationships, their occasional yet inevitable sightings bring a sense of estrangement to the feeling of familiarity. Whenever partners discover previously unseen aspects of each other, closeness is likely to suffer a temporary setback. The courage to walk through these darker places inside ourselves can breach the gap and enrich intimacy. A daring partner can strengthen the bond of closeness by offering the reassuring, comforting hand of an ally.

Fear presents a fundamental challenge to couples to know and accept or to turn away and reject each other. As fear transforms us into little children, it also offers an opportunity for us to be at our human best. It allows couples the chance to heal shame and to bring the light of friendly companionship to the coldest, most isolated parts of us. Those who are ignorant of the power of fear or who greet it with callous disdain can unwittingly abet its negative effect on intimacy. They can add salt to a tender open wound by withholding support or by reacting to another's fear with shaming. Offering an accepting, patient hand to a partner facing fear can help create a stronger relationship bond. Through this bond couples can provide each other with a sense of safety and the security of a heightened loving alliance that can help them to withstand the present as well as future dangers in life with less pain and greater confidence.

Chapter 13

MARRIAGE AS PROCESS

I've found you a thousand times,
I guess you've done the same.
But then we lose each other;
it's just like a children's game.

But as I find you here again,
the thought runs through my mind,
our love is like a circle.
Let's go 'round one more time.

—Harry Chapin*

It had been six months since Rachel and David left my office. They were having positive feelings about each other and were hopeful of their future together. David had learned to express the hurt and fear that lay behind his anger, an improvement that enabled him to get much closer to his wife. Rachel, for her part, had made a commitment to herself to organize her day around regular "reflection times" during which she focused on her own needs as well

* "Circles," © 1974 Harry Chapin Memorial Foundation. Reprinted with permission.

as those of the family. Given these basic changes, I was surprised
to hear David's tense voice tersely asking for an appointment. He
said he was calling because he and Rachel were bickering again and
that both feared falling back to where they had been.

As they picked at each other in my office, it was clear that both
were frustrated. They had each, in their own way, practiced the
new behaviors they had learned in treatment. The problems they
were experiencing were not new. What had happened was that they
had become fearful and pressured; they were afraid of failing and
were pressuring each other to resolve issues quickly. This self-imposed pressure was a reaction to the fear that their renewed fighting
suggested that they were not meant for each other.

Rachel and David's arguments did not have the noncaring
quality that typifies couples who need to be divorced. They truly
cared about each other and were trying to identify the conflictual
issues, relate their feelings, and meet each other's needs. However,
they had both lost perspective. After they left my office for the last
time six months earlier, they expected regular and immediate successes in their attempts to create a happy marriage. Now both
missed the intimacy they had felt before, and they panicked. In
short, they had lost sight of the process concept of marriage.

THE SEAS OF CHANGE

David and Rachel aren't the only couple who finds their relationship inexplicably going awry. Just as each partner undergoes
life changes, so, too, does the marriage itself; what happens to the
partners will somehow affect the marriage. Life changes that alter
a couple's relationship are often the result of necessary personal
development rather than the consequences of purely negative ab-
errations of character. However, as we have already noted, partners
tend to change without telling each other. When this occurs, the
relationship can feel uncomfortably strange and suddenly off
course.

Couples tend to be strongly reactive to changes in the relationship. As one partner shifts to respond to changing circumstances, the other finds that what was comfortably familiar yesterday is somehow cramped or uncertain today, perhaps leading to a sentiment about the uncertainty of life similar to the conclusion reached by the endlessly bemused cartoon character "Ziggy": "Just when I thought I had it figured out, somebody moved it!" But couples are rarely as whimsically accepting of change as Ziggy. As fear of the unfamiliar present and doubts of the uncertain future set in, a breach appears in intimacy. Bickering, shaming, and blaming are often not too far behind.

Many changes are inevitable in the natural course of a couple's life together. Young couples can anticipate the shift in priority from long-standing primary loyalties to parents, siblings, and friends to their own budding relationship. New parents find their tender world of peaceful togetherness quickly filled with the sounds and cries of a needy, demanding, albeit welcome, presence. These same children will once again upset the balance of intimacy when they separate and leave home to lead their own adult lives. Aging parents bring turbulent changes as needs and caretaker roles reverse. And the jostling becomes yet more intense as the couple faces their own aging, sickness, and death.

In addition to these inevitable changes, the personal development of each partner is likely to push the process of intimacy through some rough turns. Career changes, new financial responsibilities, role redefinition, and shifts in personal values may challenge the couple to make adjustments to each other. All these and no doubt other issues blow through the couple's life as winds of change.

What is it that couples need to shield themselves against the tempests of time and change? What can equip them to stay afloat and sail ahead with hope? Love, loyalty, honesty, commitment, workable communication, mutual respect, a modicum of shared success, and the gritty determination of weather-beaten sailors. Mercifully, the stormy seas quiet down at times; it is then that emotional repairs can be made and the joys of life's adventures can be shared. The rewarding trust resulting from past storms jointly weathered and the pleasures of life goals already achieved offer hope, if not optimism. Yet some relationships do take on the waters of strife and sink, joining the wrecks of sunken dreams. Still others are beached for a while.

FACING FAILURE

Failures are part of the process. We disappoint each other in both small and important ways. When failures happen, intimacy is once again misplaced and will need to be searched out. The search for intimacy lost in the fog of failure is difficult because failure brings with it some perilous obstacles that make the finding that much harder. Specifically, failing partners can extinguish the light of their true selves.

Let us examine some of the different experiences that one has in the face of personal failure. Taken in a most emotionally anti-septic way, failure means that one has missed an anticipated mark; one who fails might simply try again or decide that the mark set was simply too hard to hit. At their best, couples will do just that: they may resolve to take more careful aim and try again, or they might decide that the target was too difficult or not worth the energies required. But within the emotional reality of many people's lives—where insecurity, fear, and shame float freely through the psyche—failure can breed a nasty strain of self-contempt. Feeding off the debris of personal frailty, failure can cause one to experience a complex of negative emotions, including feeling worthless, un-wanted, and at the mercy of unrelenting criticism. Unable to stand the stench of this failure complex, individuals try to abandon their past self. When this happens, the search for lost intimacy is com-plicated by the fact that one of the partners is no longer there. He or she has gone into a kind of self-exile. Before intimacy can be restored, the self-exiled partner must be brought back home. To the extent that the now-familiar twin nemeses, shaming and blaming, enter the fray, intimacy will be harder to find and may remain misplaced forever.

In the finale of Ursula LeGuin's[17] story, our old friend Ged is returned home half-dead. He has spent the last of his energies and is essentially devoid of his wizardly powers. The world around him is caught in a kind of blackness that he is now powerless to affect. Ged is nursed back to some semblance of health by his former companion in adventure, a woman called Tenar. Since the two parted company, Tenar had married and had lost her husband–protector. And so these two companions meet again and form a bittersweet relationship that, in some ways, transcends the glories of their early travels.

However, before this happier ending is achieved, the genuine and pragmatic Tenar must help the washed-up wizard find himself. At first Ged runs away, fearing his perceived powerlessness. Later, he hides as a reclusive mountain goatherd. Finally, after some solitude and a strong measure of Tenar's loving presence, patience, and acceptance, Ged finds a peaceful self who is neither hermit nor wizard but simply a man.

With a little good fortune and a tenacity in our love for our partner, it is possible to survive the failures of a spouse. This survival is not easy. The fact is that when a person fails, he or she naturally attempts to avoid new failures at all costs. Often this avoidance takes the form of a narrowing of the former self by avoiding either emotional or professional risks. Typically this self-made safety net is unnaturally limiting and guarantees only more self-contempt. When the failing spouse looks in the mirror, he or she sees a phantom in place of the person he or she expected to see. The spouse, for this very reason, can help most by remaining as close to his or her own genuine self as possible. The firm and caring honesty of a tenacious love can make it easier for the self-perceived phantom to reach out for the substantial and familiar. When those who fail seek much-needed intimacy, an emotionally clear, decisive, and self-assured old partner becomes a healing presence.

Staying fully present in the process and absorbing the blows of failure is not easy. However, couples who do so seem to form a

stronger bond of intimacy. Family therapists Carl Whitaker[18] and
Charles and Jeannette Kramer[19] have written and spoken of their
own marriages as a serial experience: They describe feeling as
though they have had a number of different marriages—albeit to
the same spouse. What emerges from their descriptions is the picture of a kind of intuitively choreographed masquerade, in which
the newly masked spouse meets his or her mate at different junc-
tures of their lives. While each may be taken aback by the other's
changed appearance, the steps to the dance are instinctively familiar. Even though they surprise one another, there is a level of
recognition and acceptance that eases the dance and keeps the
process moving along to life's odd music.

Self-acceptance and mutual acceptance in the face of changes
and failure is difficult and often frightening. Balance may sometimes
not be restored without long periods of discomfort. Sometimes the
process demands of marriage are so difficult that the best we can
do is wait until both spouses are ready to take another chance.

Both personal growth and maintaining a relationship are processes. In the process of growth we flow from a level where we feel
centered within ourselves to another where we feel out of balance
or scattered. Similarly, in relationships there is an ever-turning
cycle of differing degrees of mutuality and closeness, and couples
may panic, as did Rachel and David, when they experience a loss
of intimacy. Yet as long as a commitment to the process of understanding each other's needs and feelings exists, the process will
continue and intimacy can be rediscovered. What's more, renewed
intimacy, born out of patience, commitment, and curiosity, is likely
to be revitalizing.

DEEPENING THE PROCESS

Actually, we may observe that there are different levels of re-
latedness. On the surface level is the minimal social exchange, exemplified by a simple but civilized greeting of "Good morning,"
which implies no deeper offer other than an invitation to exchange

greetings. Next is the perfunctory level of inquiry: "How are you?" A person using this level usually intends to be polite but also to elicit any personal news headlines or tidbits or "hot" gossip. After these first two stages comes the "activity involvement" stage, often expressed by the phrase "What are you doing today?" a phrase whose purpose is either to suggest some common activity or to get a fix on what the other is involved in.

On a somewhat deeper personal level are "shared experience" communications. These include reminiscing about the past and sometimes lead into the "planning activities" phase. In this part of the relationship process, the relating is focused on planning mutual activities, which may range from plans to take a walk to plans for a vacation. Next is a stage that psychologist Jim Bugental[20] calls "critical occasions." This is a time when couples express (literally, "press out") previously unsaid feelings, needs, dreams, or attitudes.

When couples find themselves in the "critical occasions" stage, routine relating ends and personal intimacy begins. It is during these special times that new ideas, feelings, or desires for change take place. Although these sentiments may be "pressed out" in the form of anger or tears, they do enable more closeness. Physical intimacy is often the culmination of these "critical occasions."

Finally, beyond physical intimacy lies a stage of "spiritual companionship," which goes beyond the limits of meeting mutual needs or hearing and affirming feelings. This is a special place visited by couples who have been "around the block with each other" for some time. At times, this level may have a sense of mutual destiny, religious harmony, or spiritual unity. Perhaps it is simply a vantage point from which the process of each partner's individual growth and the development of the relationship can be seen.

THE CIRCLE OF INTIMACY

All these stages and levels are part of the cycle of a relationship. Any given point is only a temporary resting place to be left and revisited. There are times when a simple "Good morning" may be all that can be honestly said. There are other times when couples talk late into the night and yet feel that there are not enough words to say what is still inside. And so the cycle goes, confusing or terrifying those who insist that life be predictable and delighting those who appreciate the dynamics of change.

Marriage as a process means having patient respect for what it takes to maintain a relationship—patience with our inevitable misunderstandings and respect for personal differences. One of the paradoxes of the marriage process is that there are few occasions that hurt us more than when things go bad in the relationship and little in life that feels better than when the relationship goes well. Those couples who live their marriage as a process continually face each other needing to understand more, eager to renew commitments, and able to forgive each other again and again.

Having a home or at least a "sense of home" is likely one of mankind's most common needs. Marriage as a process can provide this important need. When couples argue and lose intimacy, they may feel lost. Somehow, marital conflict makes us feel like we have lost our "sense of home." Finding a way back to ourselves and each other is often painful and difficult. When this searching is allowed to take place with a commitment to "process" rather than outcome, we can feel a bit less lost and more confident of finding our way back home.

Chapter 14

DECISIONS, DECISIONS, DECISIONS . . .

> *When you have to make a choice and don't make it, that is in itself a choice.*
>
> —William James

I have never been entirely sure about the adage "You are what you eat." What I am pretty clear on is that people and couples often become what they decide to be. Cognitive therapists, in particular, are likely to stress this point; typically, they confront their clients with the availability of choices in life and advocate the importance of making active decisions. Sometimes this therapeutic emphasis annoys me. It almost sounds like a nagging parent's daily admonition that if you don't take your vitamins, you will never grow to be healthy and tall. At the same time, I share the essential belief that people can help themselves stay vital and curious by maintaining a heightened alertness for opportunities to make choices and by studying their consequences. Making decisions in

191

an active, determined fashion also seems like an effective way to combat the negative kinds of beliefs and personal myths that we maintain about ourselves. Such myths might include personal scripts such as "I am not good at financial planning [or sports or making friends, etc]." A person's willingness to make decisions in areas that present difficulty, as well as the care taken to make successful choices in these areas, often reflects the authenticity of any desire to enact change. People who genuinely wish to make meaningful personal changes are apt to employ decision making in an aggressive, even opportunistic, way. In short, they almost seek out opportunities to try out new choices rather than avoid them.

HOW DECISIONS SHAPE US

Couples, too, shape their shared sense of identity through decision making and often shape their lives through the results of key decisions. In the process of making the first decisions in a marriage, significant and perhaps long-lasting patterns of responsibility are set. These patterns may well determine how, and by whose authority, future decisions will be made.

Juan and Mardi are a couple whose life together was affected as much by how they made decisions as by the actual decisions themselves. Their troubles surfaced in a most curious manner. Mardi made what was for her an extraordinary independent decision: she decided to give a large and expensive surprise party in honor of Juan's fortieth birthday. The party entailed renting a hall, hiring a band, and contracting with a food caterer. Mardi had decided to go all out and had invited old friends whom Juan had not seen in years. It was not that Mardi was unaccustomed to taking on large responsibilities. In fact, since Juan traveled regularly for his company, Mardi made virtually all the daily decisions about the household and the children. What was unusual about this situation was Mardi's decision to spend a good deal of unbudgeted money without first consulting with Juan.

In my office Mardi explained that she decided on the party because she felt that the marriage was in a rut. There was nothing really bad about the relationship, nor was there much fun or excitement. Mardi had hoped that a "good bash" would stir up some fun and add a new social dimension to their lives. What went unaccounted for in her preparation process was the fact that she ran the house on a cash basis (early in the marriage Juan had pressed for Mardi to pay all she could with cash). As the party expenses rose, it became clear to Mardi that there was simply no way she could arrange the party, keep the surprise, and cover the costs with the cash on hand.

When Mardi tried to use the couple's "for-emergency-only" charge card, a Pandora's box was opened. The store manager kept her card, proceeded to cut it up, and finally explained to an embarrassed and shocked Mardi that the account had been suspended due to nonpayment of a ten thousand dollar balance. At first Mardi was in a state of disbelief. Much of Juan's rationale for paying cash had been to avoid interest fees, penalties, and creditors. Now Mardi was faced with the reality that they were in serious debt. The information that followed was so shocking that Mardi called my office seeking a marital therapist. As it turned out, Juan had several similar credit cards, and had accumulated debts amounting to nearly double what Mardi had stumbled upon. Mardi was frightened and confused. She accused Juan of living some kind of secret life. Instead, Juan revealed that he had charged family vacations, household appliances, and Mardi's new car on his corporate credit card. He had been "robbing Peter to pay Paul" by opening a series of credit accounts.

In the course of therapy it became clear that Juan and Mardi made most of their decisions independent of each other. They saw that their decision-making style, as exemplified by, among other things, the obvious problem of the secret debts, had mortgaged their future. Each had been so set in the pursuit of personal goals that they, as a couple, had totally lost sight of where they hoped to be going. The bad news was that Juan and Mardi were faced with a financial crisis that was compounded by a forthcoming party that was now beyond their means. The "good" news was that Mardi now could see and verify what her intuition had been telling her: the boredom that had invaded the marriage was a symptom. Juan and Mardi did not need a high-priced bash; they needed to be living as a unit and sharing more together. Their lives were only barely connected, as their decision-making style reflected.

The story of Mardi and Juan is especially useful because it shows us how decisions can shape and change a couple's life. Their tale also points to the fact that it is not always the decisions themselves that can disrupt a good marriage but how those decisions come to be made. Industrial psychologists have long been interested in how corporate entities make decisions. Commonly, one of the first questions asked in the analysis of an organizational system is "Who makes the decisions?" The priority that this question has for organizational psychologists reflects the belief that leadership is a key factor in corporate decision making.

WHO DECIDES?

Family therapists such as Jay Haley[21] have noted that families resemble companies in that each can be called a system. Within the family system, too, we can learn much about decision making by asking "Who is the boss?" Sal Minuchin[22] is a noted family therapist who commonly uses the system model. He typically focuses much of his attention on fathers, because he so often finds that they occupy the family seat of power. Our concern here is not so much with exactly who the leader is. The main question we wish to pose is, Are you aware if *either* of you (as opposed to, say, a parent, in-law, or boss) is the decision maker? Knowing who the actual leader is allows for the second important question: Is this arrangement okay with you? In truth, it may be less dangerous for a couple to have poor but defined leadership than to have none at all. When companies lack clear leadership, they are prone to serious economic difficulty. A married couple needs some way to make decisions responsibly without either partner being disenfranchised.

Cary was the de facto leader in his marriage to Kate. From their first date on, Kate deferred decisions ranging from where they should eat to where they should live. Kate simply felt that Cary was more worldly (he had grown up in Boston whereas Kate was reared in a small town in the Midwest) and that he had a better handle on what she called "practical things." What she did not know was that her cosmopolitan Cary was on a dangerous life mission. For most of his life Cary had sought to get the attention of his stodgy, cynical, and hypercritical dad. In Cary's view his father lived on some kind of intellectual Olympus and hardly noticed his son's existence. Like some heat-seeking missile, Cary was fixed on bringing his father down to earth. On some level he hoped that by either fantastic success or colossal failure, he might get the attention that had so long eluded him. These hopes influenced almost every important decision that Cary would make.

With Kate's admiration and acquiescence, Cary had license to plan vacations, housing, investments, and the like. Some years into the marriage, Cary planned a trip to Europe. Instead of the leisurely vacation Kate anticipated, Cary had put together a cultural extravaganza. In place of quiet mornings in quaint roadside inns, Kate found herself being pressed through one museum after another. Whereas Kate had looked forward to meeting artisans and farmers, she spent her evenings in the company of intellectual highbrows whose main interests were politics and gourmet restaurants. Oddly, Cary himself was not having a good time either. In truth, he himself enjoyed hiking and exploring the countryside more than the cultural itinerary he was doggedly following. However, Cary was doing things that his father could hardly ignore; in a way, Cary had planned this trip more for the debriefing afterward with his dad than for the vacation itself. Surreptitiously, Cary's father had become the secret leader of the family. It was only after Kate put her foot down and insisted that they do things truer to their own interests that Cary, finally confessing that his plans had been geared to impress his father, relented.

In a way couples, like small children, need structure in order to function optimally. Young people may marry out of love, but their happiness as a couple may ultimately hinge on an ability to create a satisfying order to their lives. Simply waiting for the experiences of life to provide that structure may not place couples on the path they would choose. Moreover, when the press of life forces couples into uncomfortable patterns of living, they may end up feeling "done unto" and helpless.

Couples who find themselves stuck with burdens they have not actively and conjointly chosen can experience damage to their relationship in two ways: they may resort to blaming each other or they may suffer a loss of esteem as a married pair.

In the absence of a previously made agreement or plan, placing blame can become the plan. Whether the undesired responsibility is a financial debt, a poorly planned housing arrangement, an unwanted child, or a constraining obligation to parents or the community, blaming the partner can take the place of needed direction. Otherwise neutral problems that require decisions and solutions become personal failings with the blame flung from one partner to the other.

A sure road to blame is taken when there is an absence of active personal responsibility. Many families I have encountered expect their children to behave responsibly without ever teaching the children how responsible plans are constructed. When these children enter marriage, they may expect their lives to work out by some kind of magic or luck; in the worst cases, they may demand that their spouse cause good things to happen. Consequently, when they find themselves in unhappy circumstances, these incomplete adults blame their spouse, parents, in-laws, or God rather than attend to the faulty planning that landed them in their predicament.

DECISIONS AND "COUPLE ESTEEM"

Being stuck with responsibilities not actively chosen can cause a loss of "couple esteem." Feeling trapped may cause one or both partners to suffer a personal sense of failure. A shift in self-perception in which feelings of confidence are transformed into feelings of despair and inadequacy may occur. Suddenly, a couple who felt they could conquer the world can slide into a mire of doubt and reciprocal contempt. Sometimes, only one of the pair becomes cynical about the ability to make choices or about the choice of a mate. In other cases, the couple loses the belief that they can do good things together and falls into a state of mutual disparagement or contempt.

Balanced decision making is not an esoteric matter. Beyond the theoretical notion that young couples benefit from choosing a life structure, there is also the real and common phenomenon of lifestyle change. It has become quite ordinary for men and women in our culture to desire lifestyle and career changes. These changes bring important decisions in their wake. Changes in housing, geographic location, the family economy, and in the use of leisure time and time spent together are but a few of the areas that can be affected by one partner's decision to alter the course of his or her life. How successfully such changes are made often depends on the manner in which the couple as a whole makes decisions. If communication is open and decision making is a shared tradition, the outcome can be an exciting and strengthening experience. However, when changes of considerable importance are implemented in the manner of a covert military operation, they can destroy an otherwise functional relationship.

The couple we discussed earlier—Kate and Cary—provides us with another study in dysfunctional decision making. Throughout most of their married life, Kate and Cary both taught at a local college. Cary had previously spent time meandering in academia, his career marked by fits and starts until he settled on political science. Trying to impress his father as much as searching for his own true interests, Cary took a long time to finally write a doctorate, and even longer to land a job. Kate's path was quite different. She had a talent for working with numbers, which showed itself while she was still in grade school. By the time she was ready for college, Kate had taken an impressive number of advanced placement courses. When she announced a career in mathematics, it was in no way a surprise. Kate breezed through graduate school and had no trouble getting a tenured position at the college.

Around the time that Cary and Kate entered their tenth year of marriage, Kate got tired of "doing what was expected." She was bored and felt isolated. Gradually, she let go of the social and academic commitments that ordinarily took up so much of her time. She was feeling trapped by her own talents, which for the first time felt limiting instead of reassuring. Kate also felt that she was letting everyone down. Her parents and teachers had put forth earnest energies to push Kate along her seemingly destined path. When she and Cary were dating, they dreamed of a time when they would live in the intellectually stimulating and economically secure environment provided by a tenured position at a university. "And here I am," thought Kate, "dreaming of a career on Wall Street and sailing aimlessly on a skiff in the Caribbean." In the solitude of her "shameful thoughts," Kate began to plan and hide these visions of a new life.

As Kate increased her internal commitment to her new life, she unwittingly withdrew from Cary more and more. She did not tell him that she had reentered school to take courses in finance. Kate was not sure that Cary would be willing to support her emotionally or financially if it meant diverging so drastically from their set common goals. Nor could she share with Cary the excitement of her early stock market ventures or her grades in graduate school. By the time Cary figured out that something had changed in their lives and that their tranquil life was being disturbed, he was angry. The anger was heightened by Cary's distaste for the world of finance; he insisted that Kate give up her plans. Moreover, he did what he could to make her new classmates unwelcome in their home. In private, Cary confided his fear that Kate would find them and their ambitious plans more exciting than him. He became increasingly jealous and feared losing Kate to a force with which he felt he could not compete.

Kate, on the other hand, was annoyed with having to wade through her husband's "petty emotions" before getting on to the substance of her new challenge. She was bursting with excitement and tired of the constraints on her self-imposed secrets. As a result of this couple's difficulties with conjoint decision making, an otherwise happy and exciting juncture in their lives was strained by mistrust and anger. Attitudes that could have allowed for Kate's necessary release from a prison of ill-fitting expectations were replaced by those that caused her to be trapped in an unhappy power struggle with the man who was supposed to be her helper.

Dramatic lifestyle changes such as Kate's help to illustrate the weight that decision making can carry in a marriage. Within the quickly spinning space of a family's daily cycle the power of decision making and the subtle changes it provokes are not easily noted. Partners can forget that personal decisions affect the couple as a whole. The import of personal decisions on the marriage can make a good case for a high level of mutual involvement. In addition, a spouse can suffer more pain from being left out of the decisions involving major changes than from the actual changes themselves; that is, spouses left out of the decision-making process may feel that they are not trusted enough or that their opinions are held in little regard. Sharing that process is a particularly good way to minimize the strains brought on by the decision to alter a couple's lifestyle.

DECISION-MAKING STYLES

Given the ready logic that couples should decide on issues and lifestyle changes together, what is it that causes married people to make unilateral decisions? The answer to this question may be determined by examining the couple's "negotiation style." By looking carefully at decision making, we can see that it is a special kind of negotiation. In decision making, different needs, viewpoints, and goals are placed on the table and a new direction, the decision, which represents some form of balance, emerges. To the extent that this outcome moves the couple away from mutuality, it may reflect an imbalance in negotiation styles.

Three different negotiation styles have been identified by re-
searchers Deutsch[23] and Rubin and Brown.[24] People who are primarily concerned with doing better than others are described as
having a "competitive" negotiation style. Bargainers who have a
"positive interest in the other's welfare" fall into the category of
"cooperative" negotiators. Finally, those who are solely interested
in "maximizing their own outcomes, regardless of how others fare"
are said to have an "individualistic" negotiating style.

We come to relationships with an approach to bargaining that
we have learned from our own families. These styles are further
influenced by our interactional experiences with friends, employers,
fellow workers, and so forth. People whose bargaining style is primarily individualistic may experience the most difficulty in relationships. For them, negotiating is merely an exercise that they
must suffer through in order to get their own way. Their failure
to engage in mutual decision making is not so much because individualistic negotiators are selfish but, rather, because they are
unable, owing to egocentrism, to fully consider how the outcome
of their decisions will affect others. As mentioned in an earlier
chapter, competitors also present a problem in relationships. Blindly
competitive decision makers feel compelled to get a "better deal"
than their partners; they experience decision making as an emotional equivalent to engaging in a battle. The cooperative style,
which strives for changes that are optimal and positive for both
partners, appears to be an ideal approach to negotiation and worth
pursuing.

Perhaps the most important feature of a decision-making style
may be a person's lack of awareness of his or her own style. Even
the most loving spouse may automatically become a callously fierce
competitor simply because a decision is on the table. I recall one
such patient, who came from a home in which decisions were generally determined by what was best for his chronically ailing (but
undiagnosed), depressed father. In instances where changes in this
family's ordinarily rigid routine became possible, the children would
try to beat each other out for the "dad portion"; the bargaining
ethic in this family became "To the victors belong the spoils." When

my patient married, he would, during the decision-making process, reflexively grab for the best portion available. It was only after one of his own children tearfully described this selfishness to him that he was able to recognize that he was perpetuating the very pattern he had so long despised.

Although the bargaining style can mold the process whereby couples make decisions, it is not the only factor. Another block to participatory decision making is impatience. This is not the mundane impatience that occurs when life's tempo does not allow adequate time for deliberation on the issues at hand. Rather, it is an impatience that can be attributed to an attitude that views decision making as a simple, almost mathematical function. This attitude is often revealed at those times in therapy when it is necessary to conduct a detailed accounting of how a particular decision was made and the prospect of such an exercise is greeted by a chorus of "Are we going to do some psychobabble stuff?!"

THE NUTS AND BOLTS OF DECISION MAKING

The complex nature of decision making itself is perhaps easier to appreciate when we consider the most sophisticated conceptualization of that process. About a dozen years ago professor of management James March[25] wrote a classic article in which he sought to summarize some of what was known about decision-making theory. Drawing on previous work done in this area by psychologists, engineers, logicians, and mathematicians, March listed no fewer than eight different approaches that commonly dictate how decisions are made. These eight major kinds of "decision rationality" are neither exhaustive nor, even in March's mind, the most powerful forces that direct decisions. A brief discussion of these eight approaches follows in order to illustrate the principles of decision making and to point out the complexity of the process.

Why are decisions so complicated, and why do they require both care and time? Consider the following descriptions of decision rationality: (1) bounded rationality, (2) limited rationality, (3) contextual rationality, (4) game rationality, (5) process rationality, (6) adaptive rationality, (7) selective rationality, and (8) posterior rationality. The names alone should tell you that while we may all think we make decisions based on common rules, we clearly utilize diverse criteria. Let's briefly examine the nature of each of these rationales for decision making.

Bounded rationality is a term coined by economist Herbert Simon.[26] His concept—that all decisions are boiled down and depend on the constraints of a particular circumstance—addresses the fact that decision making is not consistently rational. Simon suggested that what seems rational when constrains on behaviors exist may not appear as sensible when those constraints are removed. For example, one might be happy to sew with a dull needle if it happens to be the one found after a search through the proverbial haystack. However, given the normal availability of needles, the dull "prize" of the one in the haystack would then be considered a poor choice. Simon also used the term *satisficing* to describe the kind of decision that is possible considering the limitations of human computational capability, organization of memory, and clarity or extent of perceptual accuracy. In other words, Simon stressed the fact that the data actually used to arrive at a satisfactory decision are limited and colored by the amount and kind of information we can consider at any given time.

The concept of *limited rationality* considers the challenge and direction of a decision in terms of how much the mind can handle. It emphasizes the fact that we constantly edit the flood of stimuli around us. Limited rationality means that there are only so many alternative decisions that can be entertained at one time and that even these are narrowed down so that we can manage information without becoming overwhelmed and unable to decide.

According to the principle of *contextual rationality*, a decision maker asks "Where (i.e., in what context) is this decision being made?" That is, this principle recognizes that what may be a good, reasonable choice in one situation might be undesirable in another. One common version of contextual rationality is experienced by couples with children: decisions made before children—for example, concerning the use of leisure time, the selection of vacation locales, how money is spent, or even diet or sleep schedules—are no longer sensible or workable after the family expands.

The concept of *process rationality* recognizes that how the decision makers get along is the most important decision criterion, whereas *game rationality*, by contrast, recognizes that the decision maker is primarily concerned with the question, What's in it for me? People who make decisions based on *selective rationality* focus heavily on following the "standard rules of operation." Knowing what the usual rules of the game are is critical to this particular decision-making process. Once these rules about how things are usually done are available and clear, standard procedures will often be followed to the letter. Lacking such standing rules can cause either a delay in the decision-making process until new rules are created or a total inability to decide anything at all. For those who decide based on *adaptive rationality*, determining the current mood of the situation that surrounds the decision will likely shape the decision itself. For those who follow this decision-making principle, the prevailing winds of the time and place and adjusting to the tastes and attitudes that are prevalent are paramount in shaping a choice. No discussion of decision making would be complete without mention of those people who fashion their decisions only so that they can later say "I told you so!" March uses the term *posterior rationality* to describe the approach that looks to outcomes and expediency.

Clearly there are many ways that we decide. While some decision makers may struggle to decide on the basis of what is morally correct, others choose an alternative based on what is popular. While some people are concerned with how everyone is enjoying the process, others are preoccupied with being able to justify themselves when hindsight catches up with today's challenge.

In light of this examination, we seem to resemble the children at play observed by Piaget.[27] Couples play the game of decision making as if they are following some agreed-upon rules, yet in reality each of us is playing by his or her own matrix of personal, often egocentric, rules. Add to this picture the diversity of our physical and emotional needs and it becomes truly amazing that couples manage to agree on anything! Moreover, even when couples concur, who knows whether they have actually agreed on the same thing?

Decisions are vital in a couple's life. They require time to process and patience to understand. Decision making would seem to be a thoughtful art, whose results reflect the efforts of the artisans. Since we are spoiled by our automatic lifestyles, it is no wonder that couples fail to be as careful with decision making as the challenge merits. The twisting and turning highways of life do not lend themselves to decisions locked in on "cruise control." This is particularly evident when the sudden and unexpected jolts in our lives demand innovative yet far-reaching choices.

Couples need to take care to anticipate the need to decide. Relationships are strengthened when partners take time to decide together and become as familiar as possible with each other's decision-making style. Blaming and other destructive patterns of interaction can be minimized by having both partners spell out their considerations, rationales, feelings, and needs in the course of making choices. Mutual respect and affection can be enhanced when the partners take turns repeating what they understand the other's main concerns to be. Both need to remember that when one partner's needs, priorities, or circumstances change, the other may not sense a shift until told explicitly. Finally, people never get everything they want in the way they want it to be given. Consequences of even the most carefully constructed plans are not necessarily predictable; as my mother says, "Man plans, and God laughs." Accepting the results of our plans without scapegoating each other leaves us freer to make new plans or hold together and endure what we cannot control or change with a sense of dignity.

Chapter 15

MARRIED TO THE JOB

Perhaps [it is] this fear of no longer being needed in a world of needless things that most spells out the unnaturalness, the surreality of much that is called work today.

—Studs Terkel*

JOB OVERIDENTIFICATION

It appears that many of us take the realities of our job, and how they affect us, either too seriously or too lightly. For some, a career becomes the sole, or only meaningful, expression of personal worth. For others, entry into the job world is analogous to undertaking a major reeducation and life reorientation without much awareness that this significant transformation is about to take place.

From a purely psychological point of view, a job is far more than the means by which people earn money. It is a powerful social classroom that serves as an extension of both home and family.

* *Working,* © 1972 Studs Terkel. Reprinted by permission of Ballantine Books.

Increasingly, we spend the better part of our waking hours on the job. There, in addition to performing the tasks required for the job, we interact with both attitudes and people. Employers, co-workers, or clients are likely to be more a part of our day than our own family. Within this home away from home, entire matrices of family issues continue to play themselves out. Those who never got what they wanted from their own family life may express unmet needs in a frantic, attention-seeking manner. Some who grew up as overly responsible, first-born children may continue to undertake more than their share of responsibilities, acting in the capacity of zealous supervisors. Yet others perform below job standards as an expression of unfinished developmental rebellions and old, pre-viously stifled angers. With so many people involved in ongoing struggles or completing fragments of their emotional development, the job is an emotionally busy place. Thus, overly controlling, au-thoritarian persons somehow manage to find themselves embroiled in conflicts with free-spirited, rule-avoidant types in their work unit. Others, seeking the approval they never received from their own families, end up with emotionally tight supervisors who are their own worst nightmares. Seen from this perspective, job life may be said to resemble a caldron bubbling with conflicts that are carried over from other areas of life. Unresolved conflicts can result in either an overidentification with the job or a loss of personal identity.

J. D.'s Story

It was our first session. (I love first sessions; for me they are like seeing a new movie.) She sat bolt upright, glared at me through stormy blue eyes, and said, "I don't want to be here, but I'm here because I have no idea where the finish line is, and I need to know." J. D. was quite an accomplished woman. She had risen through the ranks of a land development firm and eventually went out on her own. Now J. D. was a high-profile real estate developer. "I've always had a keen and almost automatic sense for the next move," she said, "and now I am frantically bouncing from pillar to post. Not only am I unsure as to what comes next, but for the first time in my life I feel that I have no direction. To make matters worse, my marriage is in trouble and there is no one I can trust enough to say these things to. So you are it."

As we spent time together, we both came to understand that J. D.'s job had become her life. Her troubles typify those of an increasing number of people who become lost in their careers. J. D. was no mere workaholic; rather, she belonged to that group of individuals who are trained to succeed and who are confounded and troubled by how to live with success. J. D. did not know how to enjoy her success in part because it did not have the "finish line" that was provided throughout the earlier years of her life, when high grades, sport trophies, job promotions, and large pay increases had been easy benchmarks. How is it that people who seem so directed can become so lost? What is it about jobs that swallows people up to such an extent that they lose their sense of personal identity?

J. D.'s missing "finish line" provides an example of how the pressures of a job can transform a softly formed identity. J. D.'s parents were not clear about what they expected of her. The single, oft-repeated prohibition was that she not get pregnant. J. D. filled this void of parental direction by borrowing from the examples set by her friends' families. She adopted broader, healthier expectations by imitating the most highly motivated of her friends. Her favorite places were the kitchen or den of her neighbors' homes, where she would listen intently for what they expected of their own children. She observed how her friends studied and learned from them most of what later evolved into her own almost spartan work habits, which became the basis of her identity.

Admittedly, J. D. observed the boys more than the girls. It was not that she was "boy crazy"—far from it. Rather, she was intrigued by the intensity of male competition and the boys' excitement with almost anything related to winning. By the time she graduated from high school, J. D. was skillfully employing what she had been learning through observation. Her status as a top-notch student and a versatile athlete offered some consolation for the pain of her par-

ents' apparent lack of interest in her life. J. D. was able to attend
college on scholarships. There her drive and ambition found new
and more diverse forms of expression, and J. D. was exposed to
some new models of achievement as well. The drive to win thus
became much of J. D.'s identity.

College led to business school, which, in turn, led to J. D.'s
first job. She had been a steady achiever all along the way, but by
the age of thirty-five, J. D. had gone as far as imitating others and
hard work could take her. When she appeared in my office in quest
of the lost finish line, I decided to ask her who had drawn the line
in the first place. Ordinarily quick-witted and well-spoken, J. D. sat
quietly; she realized that she had no idea how the finish line first
appeared. Some sessions later J. D. admitted that she had never
thought through what she actually hoped to have in the end. Whatever hand had drawn the finish line had not been her own. In her
thirty-five years J. D. had never once asked herself "What would
really please and ultimately satisfy me?" Instead she had been looking outside of herself for goals and values that seemed to work well
for others. Although she had become a success, J. D. could find
little enjoyment because this success reflected little of her own
unique wishes. In a way, J. D. chose her career in an attempt to
copy a lifestyle, much as she had done as a lonely, confused little
schoolgirl. It took months of hard work before J. D. was able to
articulate needs or dreams that came from inside, instead of outside,
herself.

Copilot to a Kamikaze

Another example of how the limitations of one's family life
can propel people into an overinvestment and overidentification
in their job can be seen through the eyes of Karen. Unwittingly,
Karen became the copilot to a corporate kamikaze. Her husband
Burt exhausted their relationship by embarking on repeated self-
annihilating missions for his firm. Burt was known within the company as their "fire fighter." Whenever and wherever a legal crisis
arose, Burt would go dive-bombing into battle. Karen would say

that she spent most of her marriage following Burt around the country.

Each new crisis was, for Burt, both an intellectual challenge and an opportunity for advancement and notoriety. Burt and Karen had been moving from one "crisis opportunity" to another for five years before it became plain to Karen that her husband was on some kind of a mission. Initially, Karen regarded the moving from city to city and the ongoing tension of urgency as exciting and necessary sacrifices.

By the sixth year of constant crisis Karen was struck by Burt's nearly total absorption in each and every case. It was then that Karen concluded that her husband not only liked the intensity but seemed to live for it. The tip-off came when she noticed that Burt was getting depressed between "missions": his humor seemed to evaporate when a case was concluded, and he stalked about the house in noticeably shorter temper until the next emergency call came, when his mood would change to the familiar enthusiasm. While Karen was beginning to tire of the grueling hours and pace of crisis, Burt clearly thrived on it. He relished telling his "war stories" to anyone who would listen. Karen began to express concern and unhappiness. When she, less and less interested in Burt's work, suggested that he decline the next crisis assignment in favor of less stressful cases, Burt was irate. The two of them began to quarrel often and with increasing fury. Fortunately, Burt had a strong sense of loyalty to his "copilot"; he made a commitment to therapy in order to try to understand Karen's abrupt shift in attitude and apparent discontent.

Once in therapy, Burt could see that he spent much of his life "living on the edge." He had received his kamikaze training at a young age: his primary teachers were his father, his three older brothers, and the kids of his old neighborhood. As a youngster, Burt would wake up each morning with a familiar knot in his stomach: he couldn't be sure he would avoid being beaten up at home— or outside. Only after he had decided whom to hit first did the knot of fear begin to loosen. The basic rule, both at home and on the Brooklyn streets was "get them and scare them, before they get you."

In a way, Burt's mentality was shaped like that of a gunfighter in the Wild West. He was constantly on edge, his reflexes ready to react to any threat. Burt's thinking was "If you make the first move, you get there first and then they have to react to you." As a result of this mind-set, there was very little peace in Burt's life. What would have been moments of calm or quiet to someone else were the most anxiety-provoking ones possible for Burt. Any moment when he was not on the attack meant that someone could be taking the initiative away from him. Burt was not paranoid: the problems or complications he envisioned, especially in intense legal litigation, were real. However, as Karen put it, "there was never a letup"; as soon as one crisis was resolved, Burt would begin to ready himself for the next potential mission.

An interesting aspect of Burt's personal style of confrontation was that his best energies were limited to anticipating and making a strong first move. Tactically speaking, he was expert at taking charge and backing others onto their heels. Legal opponents were usually stunned and overpowered by the force and daring of Burt's opening moves, which were easily his strong suit. The ability to appreciate the subtleties of true negotiation and to discern fine points of detail was so underdeveloped in Burt that he avoided those parts of the process as much as he could. Shaped by his own style, Burt had become a kind of professional bully who was at a serious disadvantage when forced to fight a prolonged or fair fight. As a result, Burt relentlessly pressed others—and himself—to the edge, where his head-first lunges were most effective. Even when placed in noncrisis situations, he would find a way to accelerate matters by pressing any point of potential conflict to its extreme. Not only did Burt live on the edge but he repeatedly sought it out: the precipice was familiar ground and, for him, the safest.

Although he would boast about his "kill record," Burt truly did not enjoy living in constant readiness. Stress had caused an uncomfortable weight problem and an increasingly severe headache disorder. However, the thrill of making the first and the winning move was something that Burt relished. For Karen's sake, he decided to try a more even pace to his life, although he could not free himself easily from the shackles of the past.

Part of what made a change so difficult for Burt was the fact that his law firm was a recasting of his early home life. The senior partners, themselves overburdened with responsibilities and governed by jealousy and greed, were harsh and abusive managers. It was an inside-the-firm joke that there was a "scapegoat of the day club." The nonsenior partners, by Burt's own description, resembled a bunch of hungry jackals who fed on each other when no easy victim was available. Failures, mistakes, personality weaknesses, or idiosyncratic habits were common targets for personal attacks and veiled salary-related threats. Burt had immediately felt at home in this environment. Part of his success within the firm was due to his hard-learned ability to avoid exposing any vulnerability and, of course, to hit first. Revealing a desire for a change in his caseload meant exposing himself to attacks that were sure to come and against which he would be unable to employ his best tactics. Nevertheless, Burt stood ready to pay whatever price would be necessary for the changes he was resolved to make.

Faced with Karen's concerns and his own increasing self-awareness, Burt looked at ways to change. He cared about Karen and did not like seeing himself as the confrontational bully he had become. Lacking the necessary skills to function without his hyperaggressive stance, Burt began to feel his old familiar intestinal knot. Deprived of his "early-knockout punch," he was afraid and unsure. He feared being unable to perform to the standards he had set as a professional; he did, after all, have a considerable reputation to maintain. Beyond that, he felt off balance without his old style and shaky about how he would relate to others.

Eventually, Burt did several things that got him off the cliff's edge. First, he left his old firm. Reluctantly, he realized that there was no way for him to contend with the "jackals" without the benefit of his trusty armor. Next, he allowed himself to go back to school to learn the more sophisticated tools of negotiation and finance that he had previously delegated to his assistants. Finally, he studied relaxation techniques and the use of meditation. These were particularly useful, since they allowed Burt to visualize potentially difficult situations from beginning to end. Once relaxed, Burt found that by forming visual images of legal problems or emotionally threatening circumstances he could identify alternate solutions and formulate more comprehensive, need-specific plans. Burt never lost his interest in challenge or bravado or his appreciation for dramatic first moves, but his courage to change meant that he didn't have to lose Karen or further damage his health.

THE WORKPLACE AS AN INSTITUTION OF HIGHER LEARNING

To this point, we have had a glimpse of how the workplace can revive old dysfunctional patterns and thereby bring added tension into a couple's life. We now turn to another way in which couples are affected by where and how they work. Traditionally, we like to think that people are trained and educated, many at a college or university, long before they begin employment. But what about the education that is received on the job—not the so-called on-the-job training but, rather, the values and ideas that are taught within the workplace. One could argue that, given the amount of time spent at work and the economic and peer pressures of company life, jobs, not traditional forms of higher education, are the more formidable educators. What, then, is taught where we work? How do the attitudes and values that are learned on the job color or shape the ways in which couples relate to each other?

It's Hard to Be a Winner If You Don't Know How to Lose

The preeminent teaching of the workplace is the "bottom line"; in lessons on profit and loss, *loss* is a dirty word. The idea of losing is anathema to corporate life. It has been said that organizations often spend more time trying to perpetuate their own existence than expressing the functions they were created to accomplish. In this sense, it may be said that losing money, losing face, losing a treasured assignment, or losing clients is often more important than producing positive results or quality products.

Through the ubiquitous message of loss avoidance in the workplace couples learn to react to losses in their personal lives with shame. As couples tend to mirror the company ethic, they can easily come to believe that their "team" should not lose. The consequences of this are especially evident in the lives of some of the young working couples I see in my practice. They come to marriage expecting to win. When faced with disappointment, limits, illness, or genuine misfortune, they have trouble pulling together. The dread and shame associated with failure or loss pushes them apart. There are often blaming and emotional distancing behaviors as well. No one wants to be identified with a loser. I have seen young, otherwise promising marriages fall apart because one partner lost a job or failed to get an anticipated promotion. In one case the birth of a mildly deformed child was enough to rip the fabric of the relationship irreparably. Human attachment and mutual affection were no match for the shame of imperfection and the unacceptability of perceived failure. These were not rational responses; neither were the people involved callous brutes. In therapy they shared moments of genuine compassion. Yet their sight was blinded by an inability to accept less than what was expected or what others seem able to have. While such human frailty clearly cannot be attributed to the job ethic alone, the values imparted through the job are not without personal impact. Sometimes the values learned on the job can have profound and surprising effects in a person's everyday life.

Losing the Big Picture: Vic's Struggle

The "big picture" was an essential part of Vic's corporate education. Losing it was virtually debilitating for him. Vic had come to his company trained as a mathematician; in time, his superiors discovered that he had a talent for long-term planning. The company needed someone to analyze trends and project goals and as a result Vic became the architect of the company's big picture. Over time, the big picture, wherein everyone and everything had its place and function, became the focus of Vic's life: it became a kind of personal emotional shorthand.

Vic was nearly sixty when a corporate shakeup caused him to lose sight of his big picture. Almost overnight, he found himself in a new city and with a new job assignment. Further, his loyal staff was gone and he had to begin to pick a new staff out of relatively unfamiliar faces. Vic was a veteran of executive positions of responsibility, and the new position reflected the high regard in which he was held in the company. When he came to see me, he had just divorced his wife of twenty years and had recently been transplanted from the city where he had grown up. Vic had planned both the divorce and the relocation for some time. The marriage had offered little comfort and brought him much conflict. Vic began planning the divorce ten years earlier and had delayed it until his children went off to college. The job move was also expected and was part of a largely predictable corporate pattern for people with Vic's skills and stature. It had been simply a matter of time and timing. Vic had been brought in from the field and was given a significant supervisory position in the home office. Quite unexpectedly, however, and uncharacteristically, Vic began to suffer intense anxiety and depression.

As long as his family members stayed on their respective courses and his material possessions and assets remained in place, Vic felt safe and content. The effects, rather than the substance, of the divorce and relocation were the demons that had been attacking Vic's peace of mind. His children responded to the divorce by setting out on more independent paths than Vic had anticipated. Some crisscrossed the country, and one of his favorites chose to live abroad for a while. Many of Vic's "things" went to his wife, some were placed in storage, and others did not fit the decor or size of his new high-rise apartment. In short, Vic's big picture had exploded into unfamiliar fragments. It was not that he objected to or was surprised by where and how the pieces landed but, rather, that his north star had disappeared from the horizon.

Actually, neither the divorce nor the move were central to Vic's nascent emotional difficulties: in response to careful and searching questions about his ex-wife and his hometown, Vic seemed to be rather detached and without much pain. At one point he suddenly teared up, began to shake, and said, "I don't miss her or Boston. My problem is that I just don't see the big picture anymore."

And so it was that Vic came into therapy to try and learn to navigate without the reassuring presence of a sailor's lights in the sky. For a long time Vic was panicked by even small decisions; he was afraid that without familiar points of reference he would become lost or make irreversible errors. Eventually, he began to use an internal process of awareness as his compass and sextant, instead of the old north star of the "big picture" to guide him; that is, Vic slowly began to learn to read his internal needs and feelings and to listen carefully to his own opinions and tastes. He decided that urban high-rise living was not for him and bought a shoreline cottage. After some negotiating and tears, he and his children decided to vacation together, rather than come together for the more traditional holidays. When Vic remarried, it was to someone with whom he could share his dreams and who would not flinch from confrontation. Vic and his partner were able to carve out a lifestyle that shifted and changed to better meet their dynamic needs.

The nature of his job as well as his own personal unwillingness to accept alternatives combined to narrow Vic's focus on a single way that things could be: only one outcome or set of goals was acceptable. This rigid approach to life nearly denied Vic the opportunity to readjust to a happier life, not to mention the threat to his sanity. When people are trained to disdain loss because it represents a poor bottom line, they are robbed of the adaptability needed to live a healthy life. We all lose sometimes. If we refuse to accept losses as something other than shameful failure, we lose the ability to live with dignity. For it is in emerging and inevitable losses that we are often at our human best.

POSITIVE LIMITS: A MODERN-DAY OXYMORON

Closely related to the issue of loss is the idea of personal limits. In the world of sales and productivity *limits* is a dirty word. Nowadays, when people or things have reached their limits, the implication is that they are ready to be replaced. In the business world the negative connotation of limits is easy to see. What is less obvious are the effects on the quality of married life when people present themselves as being without inconvenient limits. What is less obvious is how this negative stigma of limits affects love and marriage. In a way, it may be said that when people attempt to form love relationships they may try to present themselves as being free of limits. Hoping to be loved and wishing to be loving, they may try to promise each other that their love will be free of the burden of limits.

Limits and Money: Carl and His Trophy Wife

There are two salient features to the charade of having no real limits: the first relates to money, and the second has to do with how people who pretend that limits do not exist act in relationships. Consider the story of Carl. While Carl may not have been a workaholic, his limitless devotion to his profession cost him his first marriage. His first wife had loved him, shored up his chronically anemic confidence, helped him get through medical school, and left when it became clear to her that Carl was emotionally unavailable. She pursued his affection for years, receiving more distance for her efforts. Upon leaving, it occurred to her that she had "made up" the man she loved. In actual fact, in their marriage Carl had always been an elusive shadow, emotionally nonresponsive, and capable of merely reflecting the images of his wife's own loving.

Alice was to be Carl's "trophy wife." At first she seemed a great deal less demanding than his ex-wife. True, she was somewhat unpredictable, a characteristic that Carl, in the past, would not ordinarily have tolerated. Now he was able to maintain his equanimity by attributing Alice's sometimes erratic behavior to her youth. Carl even managed to view his young wife's unreliability and perennial tardiness as a refreshing change from the steady atmosphere of emotional gloom that had prevailed during the divorce.

Actually, Carl himself changed very little after the divorce. He kept the same extended hours, avoided social gatherings, and kept pretty much to himself when he was at home; Alice's cheery smile was all he felt he needed in the way of human succor. The first change in his lifestyle that Carl noticed was an astronomical credit card bill. He chided Alice about overspending but accepted her rationalizations and forgave her. By the time Carl took his next serious look at his accounts, Alice's purchases cost him a night's sleep. Again Alice explained, and again Carl was forgiving. This pattern continued; by the time Carl called my office, he was horribly flustered. He was consulting me to help him to figure out what was wrong with "this one" (this wife).

After I had met with Alice several times, I called Carl into my office. He felt reassured when I told him that his wife was not a compulsive spender. After posing a series of diagnostic questions, I turned to him and said, "Look Carl, she's bored. She can't have a relationship with you, so she's having a ball with your money. Alice is not crazy, in fact she is smart enough to be relating to the only part of you that's available." Carl was crestfallen. He began to understand how his inability to set limits with the time and energy he spent on his career had made him into a money machine. He intuitively grasped the connection between his own "limitless" behavior, and Alice's correspondingly limitless spending.

Insight is, however, of only limited value. Carl spent months fighting his penchant for immersing his total self in the job. Finally, after he cut back on patient hours, peer conferences, teaching and a near addiction to professional journals, Carl began to notice that his emotions were more clear to him and that he could relate to others more intimately. In the months that followed, Carl admitted that he felt as if he had been on a long leave from life. Enjoying his new free hours and real vacations allowed Carl to realize just how much he had been missing. He learned to set personal and

professional limits as a way to safeguard his newly found, but nearly
lost, joy in life.

LOSS OF LIMITS: OPENING THE DOOR
TO DEPERSONALIZATION

Carl's story highlights the connection between limits and
money in relationships. By studying Carl's story we can observe
how a job can seduce people away from their humanity. We can
see how money and material things came to fill the void of Carl's
superficial relationships with both his wives. Further, Carl's story
allows us to envision how easily the desire for professional repute,
the next raise, a big bonus, or the chance to make partner can
threaten the limits it is necessary to set on one's professional life
in order to protect a couple's loving relationship.

Loss of such limits presents other practical and psychological
considerations. When people on the job are told that they must be
willing to "do it all and then some," they are likely to undergo
subtle but significant personality changes. In addition to causing
additional stress, which invariably accompanies the crossing of one's
limits, an ongoing emphasis on outcomes tends to depersonalize
people when others identify them only by what they produce. When
this line is regularly crossed, people fall into the category of mere
objects. It is this aspect of limits that holds particular consequences
for couples. The powerful incentives, both positive and negative,
that focus career people on outcomes also distort human relations.
They teach people to manage relationships instead of how to be in
them. What this does to couples and families is alarming. This is
particularly shocking when we consider how readily managing can
replace relating.

Mat came to see me by way of his company's employee assistance program. He had seen the social worker employed by his
corporate office because his supervisor noted a decline in Mat's
job performance. Mat was considered an excellent manager, and
he held a position with broad responsibilities. The trouble was that

his family problems were affecting his work. Mat was coming late to meetings and increasingly tended to interrupt conferences to take personal calls, behaviors uncommon in his previous work history. In his meeting with the company social worker, Mat disclosed that his thirteen-year-old son had become a serious disciplinary problem. Chet's grades had fallen from high Bs to low Cs, and he was openly defiant and disrespectful toward his mom. These dramatic changes had disrupted the family's ordinarily quiet lifestyle. The disruption had reached the point where Mat was trying to do both his job and "fight a raging forest fire" at home.

My second meeting with Mat included Chet, the "fire starter." I assured Chet that his efforts to light a fire under his father had attained the desired result, and then asked him to talk to his dad about the trouble. As I listened in, Chet tried to tell Mat that he felt as though he had no parents at all. "All you and mom care is that I hit my marks. I'm supposed to go to school, sing in the church choir, and do my sports. Neither of you gives a darn about what I'm getting out of all this, and I've had it!" In a word, Chet was telling his father that he felt that his life was well managed but without personal warmth or concern from his parents. He knew clearly what Mat and his mom expected of him but was feeling that neither of them cared much about him beyond his achieving those goals.

Our third session included the entire family. When Lorne heard Chet's angry accusations, she got both angry and sad at the same time. Her anger was first directed at her son. She felt misjudged and unappreciated. So much of her day was typically spent in seeing to Chet's schedule. She was bewildered and incensed that her efforts were apparently unacknowledged. "Couldn't Chet see," she said pleadingly, "how much time and energy were being devoted to his needs?" When Mat joined in with his own anger toward his son's stated grievances, this thirteen-year-old boy stood his ground and said, "I appreciate everything you are both doing for me; it just doesn't feel anymore that this 'stuff' is given for me. The program is fine, but I'm not a robot. I want your time, not just your well-chosen input." Hearing this touched off Lorne's sadness. She turned to Mat and said, "The kid is speaking for both of us; I feel more like your programming assistant than your wife. We have become so routinized that I can't stand it anymore."

This was all too much for Mat, who turned to leave the room at this point. He looked like a wounded animal, hurt and scared. For a brief while he fought back at Chet and Lorne. He accused them both of using him as a scapegoat for their own dissatisfactions and failures. Mat told them that if they were unhappy, it was not his responsibility. He was doing his part by paying the bills, being home by six, and trying to plan for everyone's success. He pointed out that Chet's college program and Lorne's hopes to start a flower shop were materializing largely due to his vision and practical advice. Later, Mat was able to ease his righteous indignation enough to hear how much the two most important people in his life were missing a sense of his personal touch. Both spiritedly acknowledged his guiding thoughtfulness but longed for a kind of sharing with and mutual curiosity from him, which had been overtaken by the family routine and its well-meaning goals. Although Mat could comprehend the contrast, between the actual and the desired relationships, being painted by Lorne and Chet, he had no ready response. A manager of lives for so long, all he could honestly offer was his frustration and sadness.

There is a song by the late Harry Chapin that describes the complaints and frustrations of a straightlaced commuting businessman. In the refrain he sings: "Someone's played a trick on me," lamenting changing values and expressing a disillusionment with his rewards in life. In a way, we all tend to play a trick on ourselves. Ideally, in our growing-up years we are taught the value of love and consideration and of the wonders of nature and the world around us. Increasingly, as children make the transition to young adulthood, they are readied with other lessons about life, which have to do with careers and success. The values that were previously taught shrink in significance as the lessons needed for "real life" loom large with importance. Somehow, concerns with success and the job-to-be determine the values that are maintained. Prime attention is given to these values while the ones learned earlier are relegated to the heap of once-interesting but no longer valuable information.

We play a trick on ourselves when being first and having the most and the best overshadow or block capacities for relating to each other personally, directly, and lovingly. The security, comforts, and triumphs of the workplace are both real and illusory. Marriages often mirror the degree to which we ignore basic values for transitory satisfaction. When a partner seems to be cannibalized by the job, it is time for the couple to ask some questions.

HAVE YOU BEEN CANNIBALIZED BY YOUR JOB?

1. Where is the finish line?
2. Did both of us decide on a finish line?
3. Do we both still agree on the satisfactions provided by the job?
4. Are we cognizant of the price being paid for these satisfactions?
5. Has the job changed the way we relate to each other in ways that are no longer acceptable?
6. Has one of us shifted values? That is, is there a desire for more or different things from the job or career?
7. To what degree does it feel that earning a livelihood has become some kind of single-minded mission?
8. Are we each satisfied with the other's ability to leave the job at the office?
9. Has our home become an extension of the office?
10. Is home a place where we live as a family—or merely a depot to stop in between work hours?

To the extent that your answers to these questions point to the fact that you are married to the job, it is time to remember some old, perhaps discarded, values. Maybe some of the lessons learned long ago about the joy of togetherness and the beauty in nature deserve another look. It may also be useful to examine the expectations that you have of yourself and the job. Are these expectations truly your own? Do they reflect what you treasure in life, or have they been borrowed from someone else? In the event that these expectations do not fit, you may need to consider that they are directing your destiny and will continue to generate stress and dissatisfaction until you decide to change them.

SETTING HEALTHY LIMITS

A change from being married to the job need not entail the trauma of a "divorce" from it. Instead, the shift usually requires some reflection, setting strong limits, accepting a degree of loss, and embracing more life-giving values. The reflection involves examining the very expectations that have pressed you into such a tight relationship with the job. Where did they come from? If they are your own, the time has probably come to realize that they are doing more harm than good. If they are not your own, setting limits on such costly intrusions is in order: this simply means allowing yourself to say no to heretofore unchecked excessive demands. Examine what your responsibility to yourself is, and critically review the responsibilities placed on you by others. Regardless of whose expectations the unreasonable ones happen to be, saying no will clear a path for more time and the opportunities for more satisfying pursuits.

Saying no may affect your own self-perception more than it will change the way others see you. But in addition to enabling you to set healthier limits, saying no may raise personal concerns about achievement needs, failure, and mediocrity. You may find that having more freedom to enjoy and pursue your marriage or other neglected areas of your life also raises concerns about the areas being set aside. What does it mean to slack off your drive for the next promotion or to ease up on your attempts to ensure that the boss views you as the very best in his or her unit? Can you afford to let up or let go of personal goals that have been driving your life? Would such actions diminish your self-esteem? To the extent that they would, you may need to acknowledge that your self-esteem is precariously tied to achievement. What this means is that over time you have probably lost, or never had, a solid sense of personal value that was not tied to things you could accomplish. Maybe it is time to regard your worth as being who you are instead of what you can do. This consideration can help move you away from basing your life on expectations and toward a balance centered on what you and your spouse appreciate and have an interest in. Making this vitalizing shift from the world of challenge to one of enhancement can enrich a couple's life. This is the stuff that second chances and renewed relationships are made of. It creates opportunities for couples to spend more time sharing what they like best and what they enjoy or admire in each other. An emphasis on common interests and on what both appreciate moves a couple away from having their strengths consumed only by what they must do in the workplace. In a way, such a shift or refocusing is much like what couples normally do when they date or go on vacation, only now there's an attempt to bring these pleasures into the press of the daily grind. One way to initiate this rebalancing is to contemplate the issues raised by finishing the following five statements:

1. Maybe I don't need to _____ anymore.

2. Maybe I do need to _____ some more.

3. Maybe I need to _____ sometime soon.

4. Maybe I need to _____ once again.

5. Maybe I need to _____ sometimes.

In his literary survey on the realities of Americans' work lives, Studs Terkel[28] found repeated examples of people who resent what they do or how much living is spent at the job. He alludes to a connection between a decline in the quality of what Americans produce and their feelings about the increasing encroachments on one's time and energy of job demands. This would seem to point out that people who work have a need for more emotional autonomy and that this need is rather pressing. The more an individual's identity is fused with his or her job, the more everyone suffers; marriages suffer first and most. The quality of relationships suffers owing to emotionally absent partners who may display any of a host of peculiar job-related thought patterns and behaviors, some of which have been described in this chapter. The job itself ultimately suffers from substandard performance that mirrors the lethargy of partially lived lives. The path that leads away from the psychological addiction to expectations and toward a fuller appreciation and interest in one's own hopes and dreams runs against the current trend, but it is also a path that can lead couples to the possibility of greater happiness and fuller lives.

Chapter 16

SOLITUDE IN MARRIAGE

When you find me here, do not think me to be lonely, only alone.
—Eilleen Lynch

MARRIED AND ALONE

People are creatures of undeniable aloneness and, oftimes, inescapable loneliness. It is one of the paradoxes of marriage that even the best of relationships does not protect us fully from loneliness and that the quality of the relationship often depends on how well we do with solitude. These truths, as well as the amount of time spent alone, is something that often comes as an unwelcome surprise to many couples.

Such a surprise came to Ellen, who was at first ill-prepared to meet this challenge. Ellen and Roy had been married for ten years when he was diagnosed with multiple sclerosis. The disease took its slow and predictable course, transforming Roy from a vital and handsome artist into a sullen and degenerating invalid. Despite

229

being ravaged by paralysis and mood swings, Roy maintained a fighting spirit and a contempt for pity. While his courage helped them to adjust, his fatigue and limitations proved to be most difficult for Ellen. It was not merely that she sorely missed the healthy Roy, but she was overwhelmed by the huge amounts of time she was without him. When he slept, rested, or was in the hospital, Ellen found herself both lonesome for Roy and feeling very much alone in the world. She would wander the foyers of their apartment and haunt the hallways of the hospital beleaguered by a desperate sense of solitude. Her concerns for their future and her missing a healthier Roy aside, Ellen was facing an emptiness and strange sort of quiet that left her unnerved.

All her life Ellen had been surrounded by and actively involved with people. She had four sisters and a kid brother, whose busy lives and intermittent conflicts kept the entire household spinning. Ellen's high school years were full of friendships and extracurricular fun. College was more intellectually intense but no less social. Roy fit well into Ellen's busy life: his energy and humor made him an instant success with all of Ellen's crowd. His own friends were outgoing and definitely knew how to have a good time. When Roy's illness worsened, life seemed to enter what Ellen described as a kind of "time warp": not only did their lives slow down but to Ellen it felt as if life had stopped. Ellen began to have night terrors. She would wake up in a cold sweat, feeling that she was trying to scream but could not. When she came to see me, Ellen described herself as "going mad in a vacuum." Interestingly, her relationships with Roy and her friends were solid; it was the foreign experience of aloneness that was to be her personal nemesis.

The Scythe of Silence

Upon entering therapy, Ellen encountered the reflective quiet that is the hallmark of the self-discovery process. At first she experienced the quiet as uncomfortable and annoying. Later she found it to be almost more painful than she could bear. Although some may discover old, silent pains or long-hidden emotions in the silence of reflection, Ellen found only emptiness. She experienced this emptiness as terror. As Ellen began to put words to the terror, she spoke in terms of feeling "untethered," as if she were an astronaut "walking in outer space" whose connecting tether to the accompanying "mother ship" had been cut, leaving her floating helplessly into oblivion.

Basically, Ellen was a reactor. She had a natural sense for the patterns of human interaction: knowing when to smile or when to tell a joke and recognizing the subtle signals of small talk, which elude so many people, were second nature to her. Without someone to lift the baton for her and denied the sounds of other instruments playing the social melody, Ellen could not find a way to be, let alone to give forth her usual harmony. After hours of pain and work, Ellen was able to pass through the shocking silence of her own emptiness and began to hear her own voice: it sang a modest melody of her own creation. As her own ideas, preferences and feelings began to emerge, Ellen found a new sense of confidence and esteem. Hearing her own voice, prompted from within, gave her a more solid strength. This newly found strength allowed Ellen to engage Roy's illness and its complications rather than merely endure it. She began telling Roy what she expected of him instead of waiting to hear his demands of her. She challenged a withdrawing Roy to come out of his physical shell and give her love and encouragement. The quiet of emotional distance would return with the cycles of Roy's episodes, but now Ellen found them to be a respite and refuge instead of the mental torture they had been before. More important, the work that Ellen did in the silence gave her hope. Not only did Ellen's emerging needs provide Roy with the challenge of relating differently and more deeply to his wife but they also presented much needed opportunities for him to experience a renewed sense of purpose and dignity.

A GLIMPSE AT ALCOHOLISM:
A PUZZLING SOLITUDE

Ordinarily, the natural ebb and flow of life presents us with varying versions of the challenges of solitude. Whether it's letting go of mom's hand on the very first day of school, leaving home, living alone, going off to work, being at home with babies, or experiencing the "empty nest," illness, old age, or death, solitude has a way of visiting us all. Sometimes, however, the unexpected or unforeseen propels us into solitude and demands that we adapt to it or lose it all.

Ed was an easygoing, happy, perpetually distracted sort of guy. While some people regarded him as a daydreamer, others saw him as a big kid who never quite grew up. Always up for a good time, Ed's distractions were mostly what he called "the small joys in life." His attention would wander off at the sound of a good rock record, the sight of a pretty girl, or the chance to grab a cold beer on a hot summer day. Jody, his wife, was also his playmate or, as Ed called her, "his good-time girl." From Ed's point of view their marriage was much like the early years of their relationship—busy, exciting, and filled with the anticipation of fun.

Then, in a way that Ed could not pinpoint, things unexpectedly took a bad turn. Uncharacteristically, Jody refused to attend parties with friends and seemed to dig in her heels even about going out to a movie. She became increasingly moody, distant, and unpredictable over a period of a few months. Ed never knew what he would find when he returned home from work. He might find his old good-time girl or the nasty, distant person who appeared to have taken her place.

Jody became ever more erratic. Usually well organized, she messed up the checking accounts almost irreparably. Then there were seemingly unprovoked screaming matches with long-trusted friends. Her boss also began calling, looking for Jody and threatening termination if she did not show up for work. At home she was brutally critical, negative, and demeaning, only to later become tearfully apologetic, optimistic to an extreme, and clingy in an eerie way. Ed was annoyed, anxious, and, above all, bewildered. He could not figure out what was wrong and asking Jody straight out just sent her into a rage.

Jody was also drinking more than ever before. At first Ed hardly noticed, since they both routinely had wine with dinner and a martini after work. Although he did notice that Jody was nervous about the liquor supply and paid an inordinate amount of attention to what they had on hand and what needed to be bought, Ed didn't connect Jody's behavior to an increase in her drinking. However, his friend Gerry, who was a recovering alcoholic, did. He told Ed that while he couldn't say that Jody was an alcoholic, a great deal of her behavior reminded him of himself. Ed was grateful for Gerry's honesty and listened attentively to the signs that his friend described.

Gradually, the puzzle came together. When Jody drank, her personality changed. Before she began her daily drinking, she was negative, critical, and seemed to be looking for a fight or, as Gerry put it, "an excuse to drink." It was also clear that Jody's drinking pattern had changed in unmistakable ways. First, she now got drunk whenever she drank; she had lost control and could no longer stop after a couple of drinks. Second, Jody changed what she drank: previously content with white wine and the usual predinner martini, she now drank Southern Comfort exclusively. The last of Ed's doubts was erased when Jody didn't come home at all one night. He hadn't slept and was very worried. In the morning, when Jody finally returned, she was apologetic and strangely quiet. The worst, however, was that Jody could not explain where she had been. She remembered nothing of the night's events; she could only recall stopping at the store to buy some liquor for an upcoming party.

Frightened and not knowing what to do, Ed told his wife that she had a drinking problem and that her drinking was ruining their life. Jody was suddenly indignant. She accused Ed of being overly suspicious and railed on about how she was faithful to him and had just had a bad night. Ed countered by saying that she had been having a bad night for over six months. Jody, now in a rage, told Ed that he was a lousy friend and was giving her no support now that she was going through hard times. She complained that work was miserable, her friends were abandoning her, and now her own husband was set to turn on her as well. Ed caved in, apologized, and got depressed.

The following morning Ed called Gerry and told him what had happened. "She had a blackout," Gerry explained. "Blackouts are a total loss of memory and typically happen to alcoholics in the more advanced stages of the illness." Ed was now even more concerned: he knew that excessive drinking was a problem for Jody but was alarmed about the idea that she had an illness. Gerry's further explanation, that alcoholism was a progressive disease, gave Ed a cold chill. While Gerry's facts were frightening, Ed knew that it was unlikely that Jody would listen.

The next months were an emotional roller coaster for Ed and Jody. As Ed had feared, Jody would have none of his warnings about alcoholism: she mocked his "secondhand" medical knowledge and warned him to stop treating her like a little girl. Gerry had offered Ed little in the way of further encouragement, saying something about Jody needing to "hit bottom." As Jody drank on, so far Ed was the only one hitting bottom; there was no peace, and he felt lonesome and very alone.

Finally, because Jody's drinking and her moods seemed to get worse, Ed took one piece of Gerry's advice and went to an Al-Anon meeting. At this meeting of spouses of alcoholics, some very strong-minded folks, instead of the bunch of losers or the fatalists Ed had expected to find, confronted Ed with what they called *his* recovery. They presented him with twelve steps to his recovery and spoke with reverence of the road ahead of him. Ed was impressed both by the steps themselves and by the forthrightness and drive of the people. He was not, however, comforted by the meeting; his chief concern remained what to do about Jody's drinking. These people were talking to him about *his* recovery while his wife was drinking herself into oblivion. At the ensuing meetings Ed was told repeatedly that the best he could do for Jody was to "lovingly detach"; he was seriously jolted by this reply. He was told that he had to stop badgering Jody about her drinking and that he should not hide bottles or lose his temper. Instead, he was supposed to go on with his life, show concern for Jody, and tell her that he hoped she would stop killing herself. He was told that it was important for him to be in a good emotional position when, and if, Jody finally decided to help herself.

Ed did not know how to detach from Jody, let alone do so lovingly. At first he felt that the Al-Anon approach was a cowardly way to bail out of the trouble. But the people he met at the meetings were not cowards; they disdained self-pity and seemed to demand a sense of personal responsibility beyond what Ed was feeling for himself. More important, this business of detaching with love challenged Ed. It raised the question of whether Ed could be straight with Jody about her condition and at the same time rebuild his end of their tattered lives. The sense of separateness from Jody was both a relief and a headache. Ed had never really done much on his own. He had relied heavily on Jody to keep his life organized and on the company of his friends to relax and have fun. Now it was up to him to either quit, give in to depression, or live his life more independently. Unquestionably, the solitude was harder to face than the familiar misery of Jody's disease.

Psychology has been slow to address the issue of solitude in general and the dimensions of loneliness within marriage in particular. The clearest points of reference to solitude in marriage are topics like depression and isolation. Whereas information regarding the dysfunctional kinds of solitude is readily available, the more normative aspects remain to be explored; while we can recognize depression and even understand why people become depressed and withdraw from relationships, healthy solitude is rather a new frontier.

THREE VIEWS OF SOLITUDE

The study of solitude has been approached from different perspectives. Clark Moustakas[29] wrote of his experiences with solitude following his daughter's illness and explored some of the philosophical and experiential aspects of loneliness. In a work entitled *Journal of a Solitude* novelist and poet May Sarton[30] chronicled both the pleasures and the struggles of her attempts to maintain a balance between essential solitude and meaningful yet unobtrusive social connection. More recently, Anthony Storr,[31] a psychoanalyst, reviewed the relationship between solitude and creativity and discussed the place of solitude in psychologically healthy development.

Solitude Can Set You Free

At the center of Moustakas's study of loneliness are separation and the helplessness attendant upon it. In a way, solitude, as he describes it, is a connecting point between life and death—not literal death but a kind of end to the usual manner of being, which is, at the same time, the beginning of one's unique, unexplored, potentially creative self. By approaching the terrible barrier past which he could not touch his sick child or ease her pain, Moustakas finds a new depth to his love: "I began to see that loneliness is neither good nor bad, but a point of intense and timeless awareness of the Self, a beginning which initiates totally new sensitivities and awareness and which results in bringing a person deeply in touch with his own existence and in touch with others in a fundamental sense." In Moustakas's view, people inevitably face the limits of physical or emotional expression and find there either the death of despair or the life of self-discovery. According to this view, couples should not be surprised to find loneliness in marriage but should recognize that moments of mutual helplessness, personal distance, and isolation are sure to come. He challenges couples to not only expect such solitude but to be prepared to transcend the fits of anguish that these moments bring and to hope for the deepening of awareness and understanding that they afford survivors of the pain. Loneliness or solitude can be a conduit that allows those who pass through it to see and experience a new dimension of this common human experience.

Solitude as a Bridge from Self to Others

In contrast, but in complete sympathy, are the writings of May Sarton. In the autumn years of her life she chose loneliness. Living alone on the coast of New Hampshire, she jealously guarded her solitude. Explaining some of this choice in her *Journal of a Solitude* she writes, "It is an age where more and more human beings are caught up in lives where fewer and fewer inward decisions can be made, where fewer and fewer real choices exist. The fact that a middle-aged, single woman, without any vestige of family left, lives in this house in a silent village and is responsible only to her own soul means something." However, Sarton is no ordinary hermit. Her solitude is purposeful but also, paradoxically, social. For her, solitude ultimately means "a balance between the need to become oneself and to give of oneself." Her journal resounds with Sarton's struggles against the panic and depression of being separate from "human collision," on the one hand, and the serenity and joy of her own internal commune with life, on the other. Sarton's wisdom for couples would seem to be a directive to seek out sufficient solitude so that they never lose true touch with themselves. She holds genuine sympathy for women who mother families and antipathy for both men and women who waste their individuality in the service of another's ego. Self-knowledge as a minimum requirement for relationships would seem to be a given by her standards. Thus, Sarton regards solitude as a sanctuary of the human spirit, a place that both partners would do well to visit by choice in order to foster both their own vitality and the health of the relationship.

Solitude: Sanctuary of Self-Healing and Creativity

In the work of Storr one finds both a champion of solitude for the creative person and also an exponent of the psychological benefits of healthy aloneness. Primarily, Storr attacks the notion that an intimate relationship is the only hub around which a healthy emotional life revolves. Instead, he asserts that intimacy is but one possible hub. Through an examination of the lives of Beethoven, Kipling, Kafka, Kant, and others he argues that solitude can be another hub around which healthy functioning can take place.

Storr proposes a classification of temperaments that divides people into "patterners" and "dramatists." Drawing on the work of Gardner,[32] he describes patterners as people who tend to organize their perceptions in terms of configurations and patterns. Patterners look at life as a kind of visual puzzle whose trends hold the keys to understanding. In contrast, dramatists approach life's complexities by maintaining a high level of social contact. Children who are dramatists will typically spend their time telling stories or indulging in pretend play while their patterner counterparts will usually be found alone, working puzzles or lost in thought about various visual patterns. As adults, dramatists might be found writing poetry or novels whereas patterners might be at work in science or philosophy.

Storr postulates that dramatists would require social interaction in order to deal with the pains and struggles in their lives and that patterners would cope by attempting to understand how such events came to pass. In other words, patterners use solitude as effectively as dramatists use intimate relations to make sense of life's difficulties. Storr expands on Gardner's classifications by suggesting that as people mature they are more prone to turn away from empathy and to move toward a preference for abstraction as a way to deal with life's challenges. Furthermore, he points out that the creative use of patterning within the context of solitude can offer a sense of mastery and understanding, which can be an effective way to repair self-damage caused by loss of self-confidence, by bereavement, or by disappointment. Thus, Storr's message for marriage partners might be to understand what their nature is, be it dramatist or patterner, and not try to fight their own temperament. He might ask partners to recognize that either tendency can be used effectively and that both intimacy and solitude are legitimate ways to respond to the inescapable challenges they will face. Finally, he might predict that as couples approach old age they may find themselves more drawn to solitude as a natural need for a sense of congruity transcends the need for intimacy.

LIVING AS A COUPLE: THE FLOW
OF SOLITUDE AND INTIMACY

Contained within the puzzle of intimacy and solitude is the reality of being, in some ways, alone. That aloneness expresses itself in several ways. First, there is the inevitability of personal responsibility. Although people get married for love and companionship, they also form bonds as a way of easing, or sharing, self-responsibility. Being alone, in this context, means more than being able to live independently. Beyond the mundane challenges of economic self-sufficiency (being able to prepare one's meals or do one's own laundry) is the responsibility to determine and follow a course of meaning in one's life. This is the essential challenge that confronts us in aloneness. This is the other face of solitude. For it is within the quiet of solitary aloneness that we must all meet ourselves. In those inevitable moments of separateness from the pushes and pulls of daily living, we are left alone with our own presses and personal tugs. Free then, however briefly, from the external, our secret dreams, failures, and shortcomings flow into a quieter mind.

The second expression of aloneness is in the form of separateness. As some of the case studies mentioned earlier indicate, couples can sometimes find separateness to be uncomfortable or intolerable. One partner can become frightened or confused by the other's need for solitude because of the separation that comes in its wake.

Whether we view solitude as a refuge to cure hurts and depression, as Storr sees it, or an opportunity to confront our darker self, à la Moustakas, or the well wherein we can draw the waters of creativity, as Sarton believes, it remains a neglected sanctuary. It is often the unnoticed factor in the blaming and undirected conflicts that are so prevalent in couples' lives. This is particularly the case at times when one partner's need for solitude becomes the other's loneliness, isolation, or perceived rejection. Couples can inadvertently smother each other's individuality through the natural togetherness of their day-to-day routines. When couples have trouble with separateness or solitude, they tend to cannibalize each other. In the joy of coming together and sharing their lives, even the best of partners can lose some of the very individuality that made them attractive and exciting in the first place. Some couples don't realize that they have melded together until a peculiar strain of bickering sets in. Typically, it is a petty sort of compulsive disagreeing about most anything. Oddly, this kind of bickering seems to come and go, settling nothing and creating distance in a negative kind of way. Other couples may experience the results of emotional blending as a sense of boredom and drab sameness. In either case, the partners probably need to tell each other to "get a life," as the teenagers say, but are afraid to rock the boat. Even rocking a boat that is dead in the water sometimes raises fears that someone will get thrown overboard. Instead, stuck couples stay adrift as the relationship continues to flounder to the sounds of mutual complaints.

Couples require solitude in ways that resemble the needs of individuals but also different from them. Solitude in marriage not only affords the needed quiet and respite from the juggernaut of planned activities but also provides the opportunity to listen in to ourselves, to reflect on the words of a spouse, and to determine what we feel, what we may need, and where the marriage is headed. Couples are particularly prone to the emotional fatigue that comes from the lack of a mutually satisfying or clear course. When the direction is elusive or threatening, the marriage seems to be at loggerheads, manifested by the kind of recurrent but sporadic bickering mentioned earlier. In these situations, solitude offers both the potential benefits of a cooling-off period and an opportunity for regaining a sense of personal perspective and emotional clarity. Periods of solitude in a marriage correspond to the intervals between dates that unmarried couples use for the important work of evaluating and deciding on the future of the relationship.

Given the positive and energy-saving benefits of solitude, what makes it such an underutilized tool, one associated with people who meditate or those who are viewed as thinking too much? How is it that so many couples do without any regular routine of solitude? Why does solitude in relationships seem to carry a decidedly negative valence? Part of the answer may simply be that it is easier to blame one's spouse for one's dissatisfaction or boredom than to reflect. Marriage and relationships often bring out the most lazy and petty sides of human nature. Another answer may lie in the fact that distraction tends to win out over reflection. The pace and noise of our modern lives and a cultural fixation with outcome over process leave solitude to "losers" and those thought to be too slow in the race for success. There are two other explanations for the underutilization of solitude in marriage that deserve more careful examination. A primary obstacle to a more comfortable use of solitude takes the form of a tension between emotional distance and privacy. In order for partners to feel comfortable with the transition from togetherness and intimacy to separateness and solitude, this change needs to be free of anger or rejection. What can easily confound this sensitive transition is the tendency that is shared by many couples to use distance as an expression of displeasure or anger. Distancing, whether in the form of withdrawing affection or by literally pulling away, is a punishing club that is often used in place of saying "I'm upset with you!" Variations of distancing include "the silent treatment" (refusing to talk) and being unavailable for usual activities, such as eating a customary dinner together or making love. Not surprisingly, moves toward solitude that are played out against the background of emotional distancing create considerable confusion. How is one to understand that what was once an angry expression is now a neutral request for privacy?

EMOTIONAL DISTANCE: SOLITUDE IN DISGUISE

Another aspect of this tension between distance and privacy is the suspicion that unclarified privacy tends to raise. When there is an atmosphere of anger or disappointment, a sudden shift toward privacy leaves one partner feeling shut out and curious about what is happening behind the veils of privacy. Understandably, such suspicion does not allow for an easy transition into solitude. In fact, it introduces an element of fear into an already unsteady state of emotional discomfort. Thus, in order to avoid confusion and prevent healthy needs for solitude from being tainted with unnecessary hurt or fear, there are a few vital steps to consider: (1) Describe your emotions clearly. For example: "Right now I'm pretty disappointed in how things are going" or "I'm feeling real tense about what has just happened to us." Although such explanations may seem perfectly obvious to you, remember that your sense of things may be radically different from your partner's. (2) Wait for the emotional intensity to die down and to normalize before you get set for some alone time. The combination of intense emotions and a simultaneous withdrawal will likely create too much room for misunderstanding and more injured feelings. If you really do need time to think things out for yourself, waiting a few minutes, hours, or even days will probably not set both of you back emotionally as much as an abrupt departure will. (3) Call for a time-out as a way to gain the calm you will want as a point of transition into solitude. Once an emotional balance, however temporary, has been restored, a request for some alone time will likely be less confusing or hurtful. (4) Offer your partner some assurance that you will be back to share the discoveries made in solitude. This kind of offer will indicate that you expect your privacy to ultimately benefit the marriage and that your private time will not be used to plot revenge. (5) Set some guidelines about how long your retreat into solitude is likely to last. Saying that you will be back in a few hours, or even a few days, can help to limit your partner's pain or fears. (6) Be as certain as you can be, and as clear as your words will allow, that the purpose of the solitude is for your own benefit. Aloneness that is not meant for personal reflection is a club of distancing and not a gift of anticipated clarification.

SECRETS

Solitude and the need for it raises the issue of privacy even in a healthy relationship. Everyone has secrets. It is the boon of a good relationship to have the guarantee of loving acceptance without having to expose the raw scars of personal imperfection and, at the same time, to have the freedom to share those secrets, if desired, within the safety of a caring intimacy. Secrets can destroy intimacy to the extent that they affect the quality of the relationship. Solitude, in this context, provides the safety to bear the ugliness of one's darker self and the opportunity to find words and courage to heal those scars by self-disclosure. Nevertheless, even in a happy marriage there is a need to ensure that solitude is not being confused with a rejection of one's partner, for if the latter comes to resent or fear the very solitude that, in time, may bring a deeper intimacy, the process of healing self-disclosure may be unnecessarily and even tragically undone.

The remaining facet that can snag the transition to solitude has to do with the discomfort brought about by separation. There is an unavoidable degree of separation that must take place in order for the move to solitude to be made. This separation not only involves an interruption of the familiar patterns of our lives but also a breaking away from the people closest to us. In the first instance, many people have difficulty calling a time-out so that they can better consider and think through the issues they face in their personal lives. It is almost as if they feel that they must have ready responses and automatic solutions to these personal challenges, as if needing time and even a quiet place to reflect is an admission of weakness. These same people would shudder at the prospect of not being able to take time to examine options and make plans if a business or financial concern were at stake. Nor do they question the need of a football coach who may suddenly force some twenty million Americans to watch a television commercial while he takes time to review his players' next move. Simply departing from the automatic pace we live in or interrupting the prevailing flow can create a sense of discomfort. Yet calling time-out for ourselves or merely slowing the pace so that we can think for ourselves is vital to maintaining the integrity of an intimate relationship.

In the second instance, couples tend to hang on to any and every form of mutuality available to them. This reluctance to allow separation can sacrifice meaning and personal growth for a stifling kind of togetherness. In this respect, partners sometimes resemble the proverbial drowning man who threatens to lose his chance for safety because he will not let go of a potential rescuer. The ability to let go in relationships requires some healthy emotional development. Similarly, the capacity for solitude—and for allowing another's solitude—presumes a level of maturity. Present-day psychology has been enhanced by the writings of Donald Winnicott,[33] Heinz Kohut,[34] and Otto Kernberg.[35] Although they have engaged in a momentous debate about the creation of the psychological "self," they have also shed considerable light on the development that is necessary for a capacity for solitude. In the most elementary and overly simplified of terms, it may be said that the degree to which a person can feel alone and comfortable depends on a level of development identified with healthy "object relations." The central feature of this stage of development can be traced, in part, to how people relate to significant others (i.e., "objects") in their lives, for example, if they form positive or avoidant patterns of relating to these objects. In particular, a person should be able to internalize positive relationships, that is, benefit from contact with these objects without their having to be immediately present. A basic illustration of internalization may be seen in the young child who can go off to kindergarten and still maintain a sense of comfort and being cared for even in the mother's absence. More to the point of our discussion of solitude might be the question of how well one partner can tolerate the other's need to be either emotionally or physically apart. This is not to say that not missing a spouse who requires some solitude is a measure of great emotional maturity, but the capacity to be free of personal distress or feelings of rejection in the face of a partner's need for limited separateness is a healthy sign. This suggests that having one's own need for time alone can replenish and develop oneself and thus becomes a way to strengthen a relationship rather than weaken it.

Much of the beauty of relationships lies in sharing. Strangely, it is somehow expected that there is always something worth sharing. Even couples who are beginning to date panic when there is little or nothing to share. Paradoxically, learning secrets and discovering the delicate meter of solitude and disclosure can provide enrichment. When allowed to flourish and when requested with understanding and given with kindness, solitude becomes a couple's reliable, albeit silent, friend.

Chapter 17

THE BIND THAT FREES

This is the true joy in life, the being used up for a purpose.
—George Bernard Shaw

THE PARADOX OF INTIMACY

There is so much magic in marriage—and an equal measure of madness. The joys of intimacy are so brilliant that they can catch the eye of even the casual observer. People in love are the heroes of movies and can draw attention while they sit in a park or stroll down the busiest of streets. Couples in conflict also attract public curiosity. Most couples will likely know the peace that comes with intimacy as well as the distracting, gnawing discomforts of disharmony. Such is the puzzle of intimate relations. The mystery of the unexpected that occurs when two seemingly predictable forces come together has been called synergy. The mixture of joy and pain that occurs when two people sharing love come together makes up the paradox that is intimacy.

As the couples that you have met in this book illustrated, one positive force plus another positive force does not always result in the happy sum of two intimate people. In previous chapters we explored how emotional illiteracy, mismanaged anger, unhealed shame, masked fears, unfinished family issues, and broken trust can account for potentially good relationships turning bad. Another dimension to the hologram of marriage goes beyond these parts. Beyond each partner's emotional baggage or limitations lies the challenge of the bind that frees.

Two individuals seeking a respite from aloneness and whatever else join in a relationship that binds them in a mutual commitment. Whether the union is externally sanctioned by the state or internally stamped by a religious or spiritual bond, couples, by definition, are joined by some kind of mutual regard. No sooner does attraction to a unique individual create appreciation and excitement than the luster becomes covered with the dust of sameness and the soot of inconvenient differences. The wonder of an openness to what may be possible is blocked off by the familiar dull feeling of disappointment. "Buyer's regret" haunts relationships to some degree, and the joy of meeting becomes the challenge of adjustment. Some couples hardly notice the strains of each other's shortcomings or the areas in which they differ. Others feel stuck and trapped, like an insect on flypaper. Still others uncover the riddle and find the solution to the bind that also frees.

THE ADVENTURES OF GIVERS AND TAKERS

What separates those who struggle and bicker to exhaustion from those who discover emotional release in the commitment of a relationship? Often a process of emotional "aging" or maturation provides necessary help. Beyond the capacity to make a commitment to one another is an attitude that reflects the kind of expectations that are brought to the relationship. For example, one may expect that one's life in general and marriage, in particular, is just supposed to work out, or one may assume that everything in life requires both hard work and ongoing effort. Marriage partners with these attitudes can sometimes be caricatured as givers and takers. What both givers and takers may share is a kind of one-note capability, with which they must perform what turns out to be a symphony. The partners each hope that by either giving or taking as much as they can, be it physically or emotionally, they will be able to enjoy the fullest measure of benefit from the relationship. Both underestimate the complexities that lie ahead. Typically, takers leave relationships when they have taken all that they can while givers become righteously indignant when what they offer so freely ceases to be appreciated. For a while, both takers and givers may be frozen in the bind of a commitment that no longer satisfies. Ultimately, the one-dimensional aspect of their approach to relationships does them in. Again and again, these one-sided players will either return to the existing marriage or go on to new attempts at relationships, still stubbornly trying to make their lives flow with only a one-way approach to the game.

One key to the bind that frees lies in having the flexibility to shift gears and to learn new things. However, this implies more than takers learning to give and givers learning to take. It means both givers and takers giving in so as to get and surrendering so as to win. At first blush, this may appear to be a simple formula for negotiation or compromise. Yet even the finest negotiating skills and the most sincere readiness for compromise can leave an aftertaste of resentment. This potentially bitter outcome may be explained by understanding that givers and takers have trouble giving in to even a fair, equitable deal. They may continue to feel that the compromise is a matter of submitting to the will of the other. It is important to remember that both linear givers and takers are used to getting their own way. Getting some of what was desired leaves a hunger for the other half of the pie and an aftertaste of resentment because someone got the other piece. Even if the deal that was struck was for the presumed benefit of the children, a sensitivity to what everyone else will think, a desire for a state of stability, however tenuous, or for want of a better deal, the partners are trapped in resignation while needing release. Both are stuck in dull, barely workable solutions, with egos that are bruised or, worse, with some form of dormant rage.

INTIMACY AND SURRENDER

Letting go or surrendering to the process may be understood as relating to both individuals or couples. When an individual becomes stuck in life, he or she has probably reached a transition point in emotional development. That is to say that he or she has come to a stage beyond which established patterns of perception or behavior are no longer useful. This is usually a place in life where one must decide to accept natural limitations or begin a journey that will require a new definition of goals and acquisition of some greater knowledge or living skills. In a way it may be said that the individual has matured enough to outgrow himself or herself. For some this juncture becomes a wall of exasperation and frustration as the old round pegs are being forced into suddenly squared-off holes. Others may change priorities from job to family, materialism to spirituality, selfishness to altruism, or replace the calculator with a brush and canvas.

Similarly, but with some genuine differences, couples also reach a point of impasse. In the early stages of the relationship each partner may have had no problem getting his or her needs met. As the relationship progresses and becomes subject to the pressures of time and change, those emotional and even physical needs may be more difficult or frustrating to satisfy. Children, economic or job stress, the death of parents, and aging itself will do their part to bring the couple to a series of relationship impasses. When this occurs and needs become more difficult to meet the couple can get stuck or begin to let go. However, within the context of a marriage overcoming the impasse may be more taxing than accepting one's limitations or destiny. There are three primary areas of human concern that a couple encounters when they attempt to surrender or let go.

First is in dealing with what I've heard called the "tyranny of needs." Today personal emotional needs have an imperative quality. One who gets his or her needs met is a success. In contrast, however, someone whose needs are left unmet is somehow a wimp or a failure. In my experience, this tyranny of needs does two things. First it leaves little room for people to forgo satisfaction of needs and at the same time maintain a sense of dignity. Second it blurs the critical line between what may be an unalterable emotional requirement and a wish or mere desire.

Married couples succeed when they are able to address and satisfy each other's needs. They are able to achieve intimacy when the level of mutual caring and value allows for some needs to be passed over without great emotional turbulence. That is to say that as it is recognized that the well-being of the partner and the realizing of his or her dreams is as important as one's own self-realization, intimacy begins to thrive. As each makes a renewed commitment to this process of mutual regard, the couple can transcend the impasse and continue to flourish emotionally. It is in the warmth of this kind of emotional security that genuine needs are discerned from whims or passing wants and desires.

Second couples are able to advance in intimacy as they grasp that one cannot carry on a relationship in a vacuum. Oddly people in relationships assume that they can succeed by merely pressing ahead with their own agenda for life. You cannot be married to yourself! And if you are, chances are that you won't stay in a marriage for long. Your spouse will notice that the relationship is one-sided and will find some way to leave, emotionally if not physically. Couples need to let go of this notion in order to avoid staying stuck.

Third letting go also implies surrendering to the truth that in marriage what affects one partner will in some way also affect the other. Many of the couples described in the course of this book could have suffered less had they grasped this truth earlier in their marriages. The sense that there exists an ecology of emotions is a necessary point of surrender for each partner, but one that is easily missed or forgotten.

Compulsive givers and takers may be compared to novice swimmers. Fearing that their yet tender skills will fail them, they try to learn to become better swimmers while still holding on to the side of the pool. Surrender, in contrast, is a letting go. This letting go occurs not because the pool has somehow become suddenly safe. Rather, it is mobilized when a need to swim in the pool, and to enjoy it, has become essential. In so many of the relationships that I see in my office, the partners spend their energies waiting for the other to change. Later, when the impasse is resolved— either by chance, an act of emotional courage, or the dissolution of the relationship—it is common for a feeling of remorse to set in. "If I hadn't waited so long" or "If I had said or done something else" are common refrains.

Resistances to Surrender

Letting go, or surrendering, usually gives rise to two kinds of resistance responses. One is a resistance that comes from equating surrendering, or any type of letting go, with giving up or giving in. The other resistance is the uneasiness that seems to fill people when they allow the illogical to sometimes make good sense. The first form of resistance is fed by a pride-determined focus on what the "other side" is doing. The second is bound by a mistrust of spirit over logic. Those who feel that they must always keep score in the relationship in order to know how they are doing are almost incapable of understanding a way of giving in to themselves that does not signal weakness to others. In this way they resemble the knights of old who were bound up and weighed down with cumbersome armor but were unwilling to reach for the advantages of mobility for fear that unburdening would be taken for surrender. Or the redcoats of Britain who proudly marched on in unswerving proper rows through the open roads while their ranks were decimated by a handful of rebellious American colonials, who shot from behind rocks and trees.

If there is a paradoxical side to the bind that frees, there is also an absurdity to the way that couples stubbornly cling to the bind. It seems that, at the core, people are prone to shortsightedness about the potential healing of committed relationships. They periodically have trouble trusting the spiritual nature of being a couple. Perhaps it is so common in our culture to compete and fight that the idea of surrender without the stigma of loss is almost impossible to comprehend. Maybe we are so bound to trusting only that which we can spend or hold that we are handicapped in attempts to trust the very spirit of good intent that brings people together. Amidst this skepticism lies the committed relationship, offering the promise of phenomenon like the Dead Sea, where one can jump in with realistic hopes of swimming without drowning.

Release Reminders

Pretty words, nice sentiment, but how does that really work? Does it work? How does it work? The extent to which we succeed in finding both intimacy and release in relationships is dependent on two kinds of factors. The first set are the preparations, the "homework" of relationships, including the many topics discussed in this book. The second, the safety of the relationship process lies in the ability to express and work through emotions. The relationship is built upon conflicts that are resolved by affirming each other's needs and taking time to appreciate each other's dreams. Working through the stages of rage and anger makes the waters of the relationship safer. Avoiding shaming and blaming, allowing losses and disappointments to be mourned, and affording personal limitations a measure of dignity—all provide for increased safety. Facing fears openly and preventing competitiveness from directing the relationship make the pool more inviting. Maintaining trust, rebuilding it through accountability and reliability when it shows some cracks, and protecting the relationship from intruders, whether parents, children, or the job, keep the water level high enough for jumping in. Sharing the "whole message" of what we feel as well as how we feel saying it and formulating plans in a spirit of mutuality keep the water temperature both refreshing and comfortable.

None of this will sustain intimacy as long as the urge to hold on to the side of the pool prevents one from actually swimming. When I was in graduate school I observed a prototypical example of this piece of reality. There was an ugly couple who came to the clinic, where they were treated by a team of two psychiatry residents.

I say they were ugly not just because of their physical appearance but also because their presence cast a dark pall over the entire clinic. The reason for this was that their screaming and yelling permeated even the most soundproof clinic offices. They swore at each other and at their therapists with vulgarity and what I am told were hideous scowls and hateful stares. As the weeks and months passed, this regular scene of human ugliness continued. What did change was the vocabulary. Over time, this unpleasant couple clearly picked up a treasury of psychological insights and jargon: the old insults like "I hate you; I just wish you would die" were replaced with "Get over yourself and your terminal narcissism!" The more this couple learned about their lives and their misery, the more they stayed the same. In retrospect, it appears that they were caught up in a power struggle and were bound by intense fear and pain. Yet neither could let go of the side of the pool, their seemingly unending agenda of complaints and disappointments, and so they remained there kicking and splashing, exhausting everyone's energies to little avail.

COUPLES: THE LOCUS OF HUMAN SPIRITUALITY

Letting go, or giving in to oneself, is an ancient idea. It is the traditional starting point of spirituality. Some of you reading this section may be thinking that the concept of letting go and releasing yourself to the process of the relationship is a reframing of an old idea. Others may be saying to yourselves that this all sounds fine in theory, but how many people, let alone couples, can aspire to a spiritual mode of relating? Many of you will feel more comfortable and familiar with the kind of relating by "emotional bookkeeping" (the "you scratch my back and I'll scratch yours" mentality) that has been alluded to in earlier chapters. And tough-minded "bottom line" thinkers may be wondering about the tangible benefits of realizing the bind that frees. These reservations may be expressed in the following questions: What is the point of a spiritual kind of focus for couples? Why would marriage be the kind of place for such a fragile seed to take root?

In considering some answers to the first of these questions let us examine the current state of affairs for couples. Psychologists over the years have coined terms to describe the emotional climate that we live in. The 1950s became known as the "age of anxiety," which was followed by the "age of Aquarius," during which Americans sought "identity." The seventies and the eighties became associated with stress and burnout. It seems to me that the nineties could easily be known as the "age of compulsion and addiction." Today treatment centers abound not only for alcoholism or drug addiction but also for addictions to sex, food, and compulsively dysfunctional relationships. The day-to-day lives of families and couples are becoming increasingly impaired by compulsions. While not every family or marriage struggles with addictions, the extreme in society often is but a caricature of the norm. Today's couples are beset by an increasing number of "musts": they must be attractive, thin, physically fit, well dressed, and so on. The void of spirituality in relationships of all kinds seems to be filling up with more and more items from a never-ending list of compelling things we must be and do. If this is true, letting go (i.e., the release that it brings) presents a much needed rest. Similarly, surrender to what we have been calling the marriage process offers a potentially sane haven from the fear driven-compulsivity that just seems to broaden.

Our second question is now ripe for consideration: if our lifestyles have taken us into the "age of compulsivity," why would marriage be the place to start an emphasis on spirituality? Perhaps we can begin to answer this by viewing marriage and intimate relations as the crucible of life. Not only are couples the physical wellspring of life but the way marriage partners relate has a kind of ripple effect on the way they then relate to others. The grumpy employee is typically asked, "What's the matter? Did you have a fight with your wife?" This query reflects our assumption that intimate relations affect all other aspects of our lives. They not only shape our daily interactions but can also influence relationships yet to come. Whether intimate relations are the heart of all human activity or, as Storr would argue, only a possible hub, their influence is undeniable. They can change a good mood into a bad one or a positive frame of mind into a negative one with an immediacy and weight that are unmistakable.

When couples are at their best they radiate the benefits of sharing. In the final analysis, the sharing is what letting go and surrendering to a relationship means; it is a sharing that comes when partners each want more for themselves as a couple than for themselves as separate individuals. Both must let go of getting their own way and even of some of the expectations they have about how their needs are to be met. The desire for sharing allows partners to take their minds off themselves and focus on being together. When partners are each willing to let go of their side of the pool and stretch out in the water, they have a chance to meet in the joy and excitement of a fresh place. Each may well need the power of the other's individuality to stay in the middle of the pool until he or she is able to get comfortable swimming about. By contrast, compulsive grabbing for control or lunging back for the side of the pool will inevitably disrupt this newfound place called intimacy.

As single individuals we can also find ways to let go in our own private lives and transcend our usual state of self-centeredness. Yet there is something about self-surrender within an intimate relationship that can make taking the risk easier and that yields rewards that are more immediate and lasting. How many of our truly treasured moments in life relate to times when we found ourselves or others able to reach beyond the familiar or expected? In those special, memorable moments we are able to find a new place. Whether in the context of a friendship or in facing a personal challenge, letting go of either the constraints of fear or the limits of one's ego brings us to this special place. It is with the sharing of such experiences, that is, when partners both strive to let go, that they feel a high level of caring and valuing.

Throughout the pages of this book reference was made to the fact that two well-meaning people often do not find a life together graced with this kind of caring and valuing. A variety of culprits for this sort of emotional failure were discussed. One of the central barriers to intimacy was said to be unfinished business from one's growing-up years that is typically brought into relationships. As a result, couples find themselves in a process of both growing up *and* growing old together. It is inevitable that marriage involve a series of almost never-ending transformations. Some are delayed transitions from childhood hurts or limitations to more responsible and adult ways of self-expression. Others are the results of living through disappointments, raising children, pursuing careers, and surviving the death of loved ones. In these transformations we all lose parts of our old selves. While some lose naïveté or empty pride, others may lose illusions or dreams. We must all ultimately give up some of ourselves in order to simply maintain some form of balance with the uncertainty that is human life. Those who stubbornly deny these losses or are afraid to mourn them become psychologically rigid, emotionally frozen in their tracks. They are fighting a losing battle of trying to contain the tide of life within meager and ineffective boundaries. Their insistence on having things remain the same closes them off from their broader, more capable selves. Conversely, surrender and letting go are fundamental to life. What better place to learn and develop this essential skill than within the safe haven of a loving intimacy?

HOLDING ON: THE DEATH GRIP

In the course of conducting his seminars for psychotherapists, Jim Bugental is fond of telling the story of Carl Wallenda, the man who founded the famous aerial act called "The Flying Wallendas." In this circus act the members of Carl's family would form a human pyramid while balanced on a high wire. The family performed without benefit of a safety net, using long balancing poles to provide equilibrium. At one point they had an accident and fell, with devastating results. Years later, after considerable rehabilitation, Carl, performing alone, attempted to walk across a high wire that was stretched between two skyscrapers. (Actually, three wires were strung for this walk: a center one for Carl to walk on and two separate wires, on either side, in case of an emergency.) Holding his trusty balancing pole, Carl began making his way across the wire when a gust of wind caught him and caused him to lose his balance. In the newspaper photos of the next day one could see a falling Carl holding on to his pole. His hands were in close reach of the emergency wires, but he could not let go of his familiar pole so that he might grab on to the lifesaving safety wire.

We are all a little like Carl Wallenda in some way. Through the years of growing up we acquire our own version of his balancing pole, composed of the rules that we form about how we are to relate to, or be treated by, others. These rules are usually honed by critical life events, those memorable experiences when things when particularly well or poorly. Out of the kiln of these critical moments of learning, we form the rules that are used to maintain balance through the precarious times we encounter. The rules often vary and may include the following maxims: "No one will ever hurt me again"; "Never let them know when they've gotten to you"; "My needs must always come first"; "Never rock the boat"; and "Never give the other side an advantage." These and many others form the emotional balancing poles that people typically attempt to bring into the close quarters of intimacy. When the unavoidable moments of imbalance and awkwardness occur, the partners each reach for their guiding rules. Gripping their poles with grim determination, they try to move along the high wire of intimacy. Predictably, neither partner can proceed comfortably, and the poles become entangled. No one is willing to let go. Tragically, though the intimacy is within grasp, relationships fail as each partner clutches fiercely to the same tired, old rules. The opportunity to let go and use the love to hold and guide each other is lost. Ironically, when couples think back and reminisce on the best of times, they often remember those occasions when they were able to simply rely or depend on each other. It is easy to see the value of letting go in retrospect yet so difficult to do so in the strain of the moment. The most challenging moments of our lives can present opportunities for intimacy or the chance to forge a new or stronger bond.

How baffling it is that the very act of making love, which so preoc-
cupies lovers, teaches this lesson of letting go and surrender, which
is forgotten in the larger scopes of our lives.

OF HOPE AND HAPPINESS

One of my patients once said to me "You spend the first eighteen years of your life not knowing what is really happening to you.
Then you wind up spending the next eighteen figuring out how
you were affected by the first eighteen. The only problem is that
by then, you are already married and have kids of your own!" By
the time many of us become aware of our rules, and how they affect
our view of ourselves and others, we are often in the middle of
serious adult relationships. In these relationships our need and
desire for either emotional safety or intimacy collides with an attendant matrix of personal rules. Some of these rules will enable
us to acquire the kind of information necessary to create mutual
understanding. Others will undeniably set boundaries and create
walls of misunderstanding and emotional distance. How well each
person is able to flex and move these rules, as well as how wisely
each chooses to let go of unnecessary, clumsy ones, will usually
dictate the quality of the intimacy. Oddly, even in divorce, the
death throes of intimacy, as couples cling to the material remains
of their onetime emotional partnership, the quirks of society's divorce laws will force a form of letting go so that the final separation
can occur. Sooner or later, with this partner in intimacy or that
one, we all are taught to let go.

There is an image that has kept me company through the
changing landscape of this book. It is for me a picture of hope,
which I want to leave in your mind. The image is of an elderly
couple sitting on one of the benches that line the tree-covered
Ocean Parkway area of Brooklyn. They have been married to each
other for well over thirty years. Neither of them is especially handsome, but there is real beauty in their eyes. That beauty is in the
way that they look at each other and in the way that they speak.

They speak to each other with concern and interest, though not the intense, hungry interest of younger couples, some of whom are likewise resting on the wood benches. Instead, they speak in an understanding tone and with a relaxed gaze. They speak with ease and a knowing understanding. Each clearly has a distinct point of view, but there is little in the way of persuasion going on, only a graceful knowing and exchange. Both share the knowledge of past personal victories and defeats, of each other's strengths and limitations. Now there is only the graceful dance of positioning themselves next to each other as each gently leans on the other and moves forward. Such is the reward that awaits those who find intimacy by forming the bind that frees.

NOTES

1. James Bugental. (1976). *The search for existential identity*. San Francisco: Jossey-Bass.
2. Pinchas Peli. (1984). *On repentance: The discourses of Rabbi Joseph Soloveichik*. New York: Paulist Press.
3. Helm Stierlin. (1974). *Separating parents and adolescents*. New York: Quadrangle Books.
4. Ivan Boszormenyi-Nagy. (1973). *Invisible loyalties*. Hagerstown, MD: Harper & Row.
5. Jean Piaget. (1962). *Play, dreams and imitation in childhood* (C. Gatengo and F. M. Hodgson, Trans.). New York: Norton.
6. Irene Kassorla. (1973). *Putting it all together*. New York: Hawthorn Books.
7. Hans Selye. (1976). *The stress of life*. New York: McGraw-Hill.
8. Sigmund Freud. (1933). *New introductory lectures on psycho-analysis*. New York: Norton.
9. Sheldon Kopp. (1972). *If you meet the Buddha on the road, kill him*. Palo Alto, CA: Science & Behavior Books.
10. Walter Kempler. (1973). *Principles of Gestalt family therapy*. Costa Mesa, CA: Kempler Institute.
11. Joseph B. Soloveichik. (1965). The longely man of faith. In Walter S. Wurzberger (Ed.), *Tradition* (pp. 5–7). New York: Rabbinical Council of America.
12. Ursula LeGuin. (1968). *The wizard of earthsea*. Emeryville, CA: Parnassus.
13. Donald W. Winnicott. (1965). *The maturational process and the facilitating environment*. New York: International Universities Press.

14. Alice Miller. (1981). *Alice: The drama of the gifted child.* New York: Basic Books.
15. David Mamet. (1985). *House of games.* New York: Grove Press.
16. Claire Weeks. (1972). *Peace from nervous suffering.* New York: Hawthorn/Dutton.
17. Ursula LeGuin. (1990). *Tehanu.* New York: Bantam Books.
18. Carl Whitaker. (1989). *Midnight musings of a family therapist.* New York: Norton.
19. Charles H. Kramer and Jeannette R. Kramer. (1991). Reflecting on three lives: Mine, yours, and ours. Remarks made on May 19, 1991, at Valparaiso University, Valparaiso, Indiana.
20. James Bugental. (1987). *The art of the psychotherapist.* New York: Norton.
21. Jay Haley. (1963). *Strategies of psychotherapy.* New York: Grune & Stratton.
22. Salvatore Minuchin. (1965). Conflict resolution in family therapy. *Psychiatry 28:* 278–286.
23. Morton Deutsch. (1973). *The resolution of conflict: Constructive and destructive process.* New Haven, CT: Yale University Press.
24. Jeffrey Rubin and Bert R. Brown. (1975). *The social psychology of bargaining and negotiations.* New York: Academic Press.
25. James March. (1978). Bounded rationality, ambiguity and the engineering of choice. *The Bell Journal of Economics 9:* 587–608.
26. Herbert Simon. (1957). *Models of man.* New York: Wiley.
27. Jean Piaget. (1962). *Play, dreams and imitation in childhood.* (C. Gatengo and F. M. Hodgson, Trans.). New York: Norton.
28. Studs Terkel. (1972). *Working.* New York: Ballantine.
29. Clark Moustakas. (1961). *Loneliness.* Englewood Cliffs, NJ: Prentice-Hall.
30. May Sarton. (1973). *Journal of a solitude.* New York: Norton.
31. Anthony Storr. (1988). *Solitude: A return to the self.* New York: Free Press.
32. Howard Gardner. (1980). *Artful scribbles.* New York: Basic Books.
33. Donald W. Winnicott. (1969). The capacity to be alone. In *The maturational processes and the facilitating environment.* New York: International Universities Press.
34. Heinz Kohut. (1977). *The restoration of the self.* New York: International Universities Press.
35. Otto Kernberg. (1975). *Borderline conditions and pathological narcissism.* New York: Jason Aronson.

INDEX